American POWs in Korea

American POWs in Korea

Sixteen Personal Accounts

Edited by HARRY SPILLER

McFarland & Company, Inc., Publishers
Jefferson, North Carolina, and London

Cover: The POWs inside their compound in Enclosure #2, POW Camp #1, Koje-Do. U.S. Army photo by Private Allen Johnson, August 29, 1953.

British Library Cataloguing-in-Publication data are available

Library of Congress Cataloguing-in-Publication Data

Spiller, Harry, 1945–
    American POWs in Korea : sixteen personal accounts / edited by
Harry Spiller.
        p.   cm.
    Includes index.
    ISBN 0-7864-0561-9 (sewn softcover : 50# alkaline paper) ∞
    1. Korean War. 1950–1953—Prisoners and prisons, American.
    2. Prisoners of war—Korea (North)   3. Korean War, 1950–1953
    —Personal narratives, American.   I. Title.
    DS921.S65   1998
    951.904'27—dc21   98-14205
                                                                      CIP

Manufactured in the United States of America

*McFarland & Company, Inc., Publishers
    Box 611, Jefferson, North Carolina 28640*

This book is dedicated to
all the ex–prisoners of war in Korea
and their families

ACKNOWLEDGMENTS

I would like to thank Robin Greenlee and Michael Dann for their artwork. Also, for sharing their experiences, I wish to thank the ex–POWs who made this book possible.

CONTENTS

INTRODUCTION

During a monsoon rain in the early morning hours of June 25, 1950, the North Korean People's Army crossed the 38th parallel into South Korea. The northern army, much larger, better trained, and better equipped, quickly swarmed southward. The South Korean Army, outgunned and overwhelmed, was left in total confusion.

The United States compared the actions by the North Korean Communist aggressors to those of Hitler, Mussolini, and the Japanese during World War II. Six days later President Truman committed American troops to Korea in what he called a "police action."

The public was given three explanations about the commitment to the war. The first was that there was a civil war between the north and south; the second, that there was a collective effort by the United Nations to stop a treaty-breaking aggressor; and the third, that the Western countries were blocking the expansion of Communist aggression. Regardless of the explanation, it would become obvious that this was anything but a "police action." Over the next three years and one month, 172,897 American troops would fight in Korea, with a total of 54,246 killed, 103,284 wounded, and 8,177 missing in action.

The distress of combat is horrible, but the distress from cruelty and suffering endured by the prisoners of war goes beyond the reach of the imagination. During the Korean War there were 7,190 Americans captured. The U.S. Army bore the largest burden with 6,656; the air force was next with 263; followed by the marines with 231; and finally the navy with 40. The prisoners of war were incarcerated in 20 camps located in North Korea. Of the 7,190 Americans captured, 2,701 died in captivity. That is more than one in three, or nearly 40 percent. Many of those who died were brutally murdered or starved to death, or they died from lack of medical treatment or from severe cold.

There were three general time periods of captivity. The first started with capture and ended in the first permanent camp. During this period the prisoners were denied food and shelter and forced to participate in long marches, often lasting for weeks. These were later to become known as the death marches.

The POWs, their hands often tied behind their backs with communications wire, were forced to march without food or water. They marched through snowstorms without adequate clothing, and some had no boots. Frostbite and other injuries were common. Dysentery became an ever-present problem, with no medical treatment available. Many of the POWs developed pneumonia.

In addition, the captors took revenge on the American POWs for air raids by Americans during the marches. On one occasion a POW reported seeing 26 of his fellow prisoners lined up with their hands tied behind their backs and mowed down with machine guns after the Americans strafed the area. On another occasion 100 prisoners were found murdered on a train in a tunnel where the train had hidden from American air surveillance.

As an example of the death tolls on these marches, consider a march that began on March 13, 1951, en route to Camp Five. The march ended on March 19 with only 109 of the original 250–300 prisoners alive. It is likely that most of the 8,177 reported missing in action died in captivity on the way to permanent camps in North Korea.

The second time period began at the first permanent camp and ended about October 1951. The prisoners were denied all necessities of life. The food was grossly inadequate. The sanitation and hygiene were horrible. There was no medical treatment. The men were housed in unheated Korean farmhouses infested with body lice and other vermin. Sickness and death became the daily routine.

The third period began after October 1951, and the conditions depended on the political situation and the feelings toward the armistice conference. There were gradual increases in food, clothing, and medicine, but the diet remained inadequate in protein and vitamin content. The housing was improved with some comforts, and the clothing was adequate for survival. Medical care was never adequate.

The one marked difference in the treatment of the POWs in Korea, compared with POWs in other wars, was the Communist indoctrination. The purpose of the indoctrination was to force prisoners to accept Communist ideology and to neutralize them as a threat. The first step in indoctrination was to break down the normal resistance by keeping the prisoners cold, hungry, and in a state of confusion. The second step consisted of formal study programs, following the theme that the United States was imperialistic, with a few rich people running the country, and that Communist doctrine reflected the aims of all the people. During this phase of indoctrination, clothing and food were improved. The third step consisted of small group interviews, with the intent of finding different individual views on issues such as race, religion, or economic status.

The Communists, for the most part, were unsuccessful at the indoctrination. Only 21 prisoners accepted the Communist ideology. The second purpose of the indoctrination, group neutralization, was somewhat more successful. The Communists were able to foster discontent and distrust among the prisoners, which damaged the unity of the prisoners and created a lack of effective resistance against the Communists.

The prisoners of war in Korea had no training in what to do if they were captured. They had no preparation for the stresses of political indoctrination. Yet their ability to endure, to live with isolation, cold, hunger, and disease, was as superhuman as their treatment was inhuman.

I could go on and on about the conditions and treatment of prisoners of war in Korea, but the best way to give a true picture of their daily life is through individual stories of men who were prisoners of war. This book contains 16 personal accounts of men who fought the North Koreans and Chinese Communists only to face the grim reality of life as a POW.

As a child I saw news stories of men fighting in Korea. I can remember my father and my draft-age brother discussing the possibility of induction. In later years I developed an interest about the events of the Korean War, and that interest became the inspiration for this book.

The information in this book came from personal interviews with ex–prisoners of war; personal documents from ex–prisoners of war; military records from the National Archives in Washington, D.C., the National Headquarters of Ex–prisoners of War in Texas, and the War Department in Washington, D.C.; and from two books: *Korean War Ex–Prisoners of War* (Paducah, Ky.: Turner, 1993), and *The Forgotten War ... Remembered* (Paducah, Ky.: Turner, 1993).

The stories in this book are real, they are compelling, and they give a true picture of life as a prisoner of war in Korea.

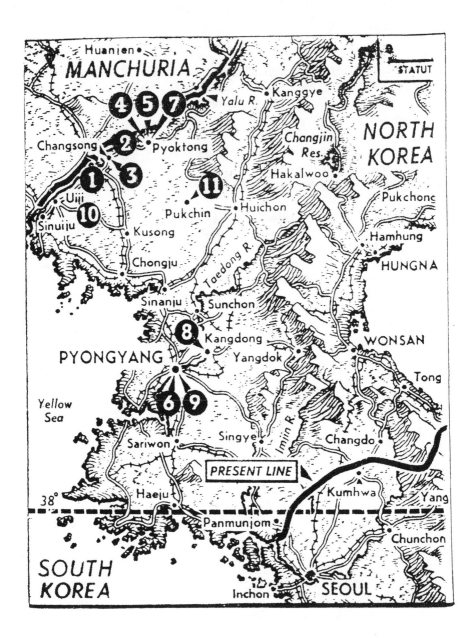

Prison camp locations as reported by U.N. intelligence early in the war. 1. Changsong. 2. Pyoktong. 3. Changsong. 4. Pyoktong. 5. Pyoktong. 6. Pyongyang. 7. Pyoktong. 8. Kangdong. 9. Pyongyang. 10. Chon-Ma. 11. Pukchin. As the war continued, camps were added, and names and locations changed. For this reason, camps shown on this map may differ from descriptions of camps elsewhere in this book.

– 1 –

PRIVATE FIRST CLASS
DONALD M. ELLIOTT
U.S. ARMY

Headquarters Company, 38th Infantry, 2nd Division
Captured During a Counter-Attack at the 38th Parallel
Prisoner of War
May 18, 1951–August 20, 1953
Mining and Bean Camp, Camp One

The Draft: Infantry Basic Training, November 27, 1950

Don was drafted into the U.S. Army on November 27, 1950. His first experiences as a soldier were at Fort Leonard Wood, Missouri, where he took his infantry combat training. The new life in the military was filled with close order drill, exercise, rifle ranges, exercise, inspections, hand-to-hand combat training, and exercise. Upon completion of training, Don was assigned to Fort Lewis, Washington, with the 38th Infantry, 2nd Division. The 38th Infantry was supervising training and summer camp when the North Koreans crossed the 38th parallel and invaded the Republic of South Korea.

The Korean War: A Call to Duty, July 1950–August 1950

Don's unit was placed on alert on July 9, 1950, and it departed for Tacoma, Washington, on August 5, 1950. The unit begin arriving on August 19 in Pusan, Korea. The first duty of the 38th Infantry was to defend a stretch of the Naktong River. The unit repelled a fierce attack by the Chinese in late August. From that time until April 1951, Don's unit was involved in numerous defense positions and battles.

From late August through September, the unit took Hill G285, Hill 115, and Hill 208. In October they became Task Force Indianhead and set up blocking

5

positions near Pyongyang, Suchon, and Yongdon-ni. In November they engaged in an offensive advancing west of Tougchong. The 38th Regiment suffered severe casualties fighting through roadblocks south of Kunu-ri. They stopped at Han River. In January 1951 the unit moved from Han River, and from that time until April they were involved in Operation Killer, designed to push the Chinese Communist forces north of Han River.

Then in March they were part of Operation Ripper, with the purpose of pushing the Communists back to the 38th parallel. In May the unit was counterattacked by the Chinese, and the entire division withdrew to line No-Name. Don's unit was overrun, and he was captured by the Chinese soldiers.

The Battle and Capture: May 18, 1951

Don's unit was just below the 38th parallel near the town of Kari San. He was located in the battalion rear working as a switchboard operator in the communications section of Headquarters Company. On May 18 the Chinese, with 80,000 troops, made a counterattack south. The South Korean troops were on the eastern point of the defense line when the Chinese hit. When the fighting got intense, the Korean troops retreated. The Chinese sent troops to the rear of the defense line and then attacked from the front, rear, and eastern flank. Don and his unit were 2,000 strong against 80,000 Chinese. Don recalled:

At about 2:00 A.M. when I was relieved from the switchboard, I made a trip out of the switchboard area. The switchboard was a trench and dugout area into the side of a rice paddy with a shelter-half hanging over the entrance. I went to the latrine. As I returned to the dugout I realized the Chinese troops were in our area. I started running. I tripped over something on the ground and fell flat on my face. That no doubt was the most fortunate fall I ever had because as I started to get up a Chinese fired about ten rounds at me. I ended up with a face full of dirt but not hit. After lying a short while and looking around, I continued on crawling the 20 yards or so back to the dugout. The next adventure was only about four hours later. The switchboard crew was joined during the night by two of our battalion-forward communications detachment men who had been caught in a firefight and had been sent back to the rear for a good night's sleep. We also had some South Korean supply people in the bunker. They had been hired by the army to carry supplies from regiment headquarters to points forward. When sunrise came I became aware of a Korean supply carrier sitting right next to me. I didn't know if he was Korean or Chinese so for probably 30 minutes my bayonet was a few inches from his ribs. Had he turned out to be Chinese, I was prepared to shove the bayonet into him.

After daylight, it became obvious that we were surrounded. For a couple of hours the Chinese were running through the area. One of them had a trumpet and played taps on it over and over for an hour. I was on the telephone with the battalion executive major when he bought the farm from a machine gun. At 6:10 A.M. a burst of burp gun was fired through the shelter-half that covered the entrance to our dugout-switchboard area. I guess I will always remember the circle pattern of the burp gun blast. There were nine rounds fired, there were nine people in the dugout, and the Korean beside me got all nine rounds. He didn't even moan.

Immediately the two men from battalion forward started calling out "surrender" and "prisoner." They then started filing out of the dugouts with their hands in the air. Because I was the person on duty I was sitting the farthest from the entrance and was the last to leave. Immediately after we filed out of the dugout a North Korean soldier wanted to shoot all eight of us. The Chinese troops actually jerked his weapon away and booted the N.K. in the behind and sent him away from us.

I guess I was lucky as compared to some. Jim O'Boyle from a different outfit was captured on May 15 in a firefight. He was held by the Chinese for three days before being brought south during their big push. The Chinese told him to keep going when they crossed our original defense line. He checked in at headquarters rear. Someone handed him a rifle and sent him forward. He spent part of the night with us before being captured along with the rest of us. It was the second time he had been captured in three days. Jim died of diphtheria in February 1952 while in Camp Three.

Captivity

The March: May 18, 1951–October 8, 1951. They captured about 800 troops from all companies of the 2nd Division. Because of the large number of POWs we were constantly moving from place to place trying to find enough food. We spent the first night in an abandoned Korean hut while we waited for more and more POWs to be assembled. The second night we spent in a cave with very little air. We went in after dark, and there wasn't enough air to burn a match. The rumor circulated that the entrance to the cave was going to be closed off and we were all going to die. But it was just a rumor.

About noon the next day the Chinese started taking us out of the caves. The UN Air Force was conducting an air strike in the region. In groups of four and five we had to crawl out of the cave and then run about 50 yards to a forest area for protection from the bombs. We walked and carried the wounded for days. There was little food, and some of the men were wounded badly. As we marched they just wasted away, and within the first eight days men started dying—one or two a day. We made our way north, mostly walking at night and resting anyplace we could find during the day. It was May 30 and we were walking in the early evening. It started raining real hard. I was a long way from the front line and I didn't see what happened, but the story that circulated went like this. The lead guard stopped to ask directions of either a Korean or another Chinese soldier and was told we should stay to the right at a Y in the path. We spent all night slipping and falling and trying to climb a very high mountain in the rain. The next morning when it quit raining and we couldn't find our destination we were told we took the wrong trail the night before. At that point the guards were either very tired themselves or showed some compassion for the conditions because we rested for a full 24 hours before we retraced our steps and crossed the mountains going the other way to return to the spot where we took the wrong turn.

One very helpful incident occurred near the end of the return trip: an officer of the Chinese army passed out and was lying beside the trail as we all walked past. That was a real morale booster. The GIs started singing marching songs and managed to stay happy for a few hours. The guards were happy that we were happy but didn't have a clue for the reason.

We walked for about three or four weeks and those of us who were left finally made it to the first stop—the Bean Camp.

The Bean Camp. Our first extended stop was at the Bean Camp. The camp got the name because of the diet—almost exclusively they fed us soybeans. We thought our diet had improved when we got to the camp because of the soybean diet. Up until that time we had been eating bug dust," a millet or sorghum grain with kidney beans in the sorghum. Bug dust is a very fine powder made up of the brown outer shell of rice when it is polished to make it like the rice we are familiar with. Later we found out that soy beans must be boiled for several hours to break down the hard outer shell. The Chinese either didn't know or didn't care or didn't have the time properly to cook the soy beans. The improperly cooked soybeans will pass through the digestive system very rapidly and in the process tear up everything on the way. Within two days every POW had diarrhea or dysentery. When my dysentery started, I quit eating the beans and just used the liquid they were cooked in. We stayed at the Bean Camp for three or four weeks before we started marching again. By the time we left I had gotten rid of my dysentery, but many of the GIs hadn't. When we started to march again they were too weak and they'd started dying.

The Mining Camp. We arrived at the Mining Camp on July 3, 1951. With the exception of about one death per day and the bastard doctor who sold the little bit of medicine he was given to care for us, things were much better at this camp. We had a roof over our heads and enough room to lie down to sleep. The food improved some, with occasional rice and canned meat.

At the Bean Camp the Chinese had started a little bit of indoctrination, but when we got to the Mining Camp indoctrination was held every day. It was the good of all the people with Communism, and capitalism was for the few rich. No one was taking it seriously. Then, after a couple of months, on September 20, 1951, the Chinese moved us again.

Camp One: October 1951–August 1953. The Chinese army moved the civilians out of their homes, and we moved in. The town was Chon Chin, a good-sized town. We were issued student uniforms and had an opportunity to wash clothes and get rid of the lice we had been living with since about June of '51. The lice eggs needed body heat to hatch, so as soon as we were able to wash clothes and get them off our bodies the new lice quit hatching and we were able to live without lice.

There were about 30 huts, with two to three rooms each and ten GIs per room. The rooms were about 10 by 15 feet. We ate, slept, spent all our time this way. The only change was "brainwashing" sessions and a few work details. Most of those were gathering firewood for heating and cooking. We also had about 100 British troops across the road. No fences.

The guards experienced night blindness starting about November and lasting until late April when we started eating fresh vegetables again. Many of the POWs also had night blindness because of poor diet with little or zero vegetables.

Regardless of how bad things are for a person you can always find someone who has it worse. I was near the Chinese kitchen and saw a blind Korean woman trying to find food for her self and a naked baby that was about nine months old. She was sitting in the garbage pile sifting through the garbage with her hands. Because of her blindness every little piece she picked up had to go to her nose and mouth for sampling. After the test, if she thought it was of some value it went into a very small gourd bowl. If she didn't think it was edible, it went back into the pile. It was a heart-breaking sight, but one that helped me because I actually realized that even though I was a prisoner of war I was lucky compared with her.

In 1952 the peace talks were going well and things in the camp began to get better. The medical care improved enough that if someone got sick and went to sick call and ended up in the hospital we didn't tell them good-bye. Prior to this the sick and wounded simply died if the other GIs couldn't take care of them. A few died after 1952 but not like before. As best that we could figure, of the approximately 800 captured between May 18, 1950, and May 20, 1951, 54 percent died as a result of wounds or dysentery while we were marching from place to place trying to find enough food.

I had two incidents that happened to me with the doctors. The first incident happened in February 1952 when I came down with a deep chest cold. Always, when I had a chest cold when I was younger, asthma was not far behind. The asthma came this time, but by now we had sick call in the camp. Because I had had a life-long problem with asthma I had a good idea how it should be controlled. I went to sick call and explained to the doctor what my treatment should be. The doctor had heard of asthma but had never treated anyone. I explained that first we must treat the cold, then, to relieve the symptoms of the asthma, adrenaline-in-oil would relieve the wheezing. To my surprise he provided the sulfa drug for the cold and further, he advised that he didn't have the adrenaline but he would get it. We talked for 30–45 minutes. I felt like he had a sincere interest in my problem and was very much wanting to learn from me about asthma. The sulfa did its job in about three days, and then for the next two days he called me to sick call to administer the adrenaline. The combination worked, and I was careful not to catch a cold again.

The second incident dealt with the general condition of my body. We were eating only two meals a day at the time, and I had been having diarrhea for about six months. The diet was vastly different from what GIs were accustomed to eating, and nearly everyone had some problems with their digestive systems, not to mention all the other problems too numerous to describe. During one very cold spell, 40–50 degrees below zero, my diarrhea got much worse. During the 24-hour period, I made 32 trips to the outhouse. It was outside and about 20 feet from our hut. The diarrhea improved, but these trips in the cold plus the lack of heat in the hut took their toll on us. About two or three weeks later, they let me have some water and I tried to clean up a little. I took off my shoes and socks and discovered three frozen toes. They were black on the ends. I went to sick call thinking I was going to lose my toes. Instead, the doctor started scraping the ends of my toes. I started sick call visits each day, and a nurse would put on a black tarlike substance on my toes to draw out the infection. Every other visit they would put sulfur powder on my toes to heal them. It worked. By the time the infection was gone my toes were healed. Very primitive, but it worked. A side benefit of all this was that the Chinese cooks got a big cast-iron pot, put it in our kitchen, and we had heat. They and our cooks used the hot water to cook.

If you were quiet enough you could walk by the guards because of the poor eyesight, so a few GIs were shot or shot at during the November–April time periods. The turnips helped everyone's night blindness, and after that the guards weren't so jumpy.

At this camp the indoctrination increased to twice a day, except during the cold weather. The most concentrated effort took place in late summer through fall of 1952. They tried very hard to convince us that the U.N. troops were using germ warfare. They set up a display of bugs, bomb fragments, and pictures to convince us. We had about five or six weeks of this constant preaching about germ warfare, then we saw the display, and finally we took a written test to see how much we had learned. We heard a rumor that in Camp Five one of the prisoners swallowed one of the bugs and the Chinese starved him for two weeks to be sure he got sick, but they finally gave up. He was really hungry, but he didn't get sick.

After we took the test about germ warfare, the Chinese were unhappy with our lack of learning and stopped most of the brainwashing. One of the interpreters called me to headquarters to ask why I didn't believe that germ warfare had been used. I told him if our military were using germ warfare we would all be dead. He told me I had a bad attitude and sent me back to my hut.

In the spring of 1952 we asked for vegetables, and the Chinese got a truckload of turnips. We had 101 meals of boiled turnips (two meals a day for 50 days).

By 1953, things continued to improve. The living conditions, diet, and the opportunity to play a little baseball were part of it. One of the things that always amazed me was how much difficulty two different cultures can have communicating. I can remember an incident that is funny now, but it wasn't at the time. The Chinese were constantly accusing us of crimes against the common people's republic. As a consequence of this, various GIs were suddenly arrested, and as a result of these arrests they usually were moved away from our camp. We seldom ever saw the arrested person again. One evening in the early spring of '53 at an evening formation the camp commander, whom we rarely saw, announced the arrest of Donald … Bittner, for crimes undisclosed. I and all the others with the first name of Donald had a uh-oh feeling as the interpreter paused between the first and last name for at least 15 seconds. Bittner was arrested and removed from the formation, never to be seen in our camp again. After the formation broke up, we all returned to our squad rooms. Joe Bramantti, a big mouth, called to me from two rooms away: "Well, they almost got you this time, didn't they?" I didn't say much because just at about that time we became aware that one of the interpreters was standing outside the door listening to our babble. At 3:00 A.M. a guard came after me. I will always believe it was because of Joe's wisecrack, but what we will never know is why the guard was there in the first place. For the next three days I learned a lot about what was going on around the camp. First, the Chinese believed that I and my followers had burned down the rec-room they had just built for us. Someone threw a rock through the window of the Chinese headquarters telling the Chinese that they had better shape up or be shipped out. Several other incidents were supposed to have happened, according to the Chinese, and I was supposed to be the ringleader of it all. Several others had been arrested and were suspected as ringleaders also. I was questioned and accused by a Chinese officer for several hours. The officer drank tea and smoked constantly as he questioned me, and then suddenly he left the room with papers scattered all over his desk. Very strangely, of all the papers on the desk there was only one in English. I asked myself why a Chinese interpreter would leave that paper if he didn't want me to read it. Well, I read it. It was a list of bad guys in my group. All these guys were the people who had been arrested and removed from camp in the last year or so, including Don Bittner. I will never know if my confession was better than the rest, but I was not arrested and removed from the camp like the rest

Top: An aerial photo of POW Compound #13, POW Camp #1, East Valley, Koje-Do. U.S. Army photo, April 13, 1953. *Bottom:* A typical latrine with washing facilities in the center of the room at U.N. POW Camp #1. U.S. Army photo, December 11, 1952.

of the so-called bad guys had been. When the Chinese interpreter returned, he told me that I should stand at attention and consider the error of my ways and my crimes against the common people's republic. I considered it at attention for 34 hours straight. At the end of that time I was given a paper and pen and told to write my confession. The first attempt took three or four hours and involved about four pages. I did not implicate anyone except the others on the list and only wrote in generalities about the crimes against the people. After my first attempt I was offered a cigarette and tea. I took the tea, but refused the cigarette and it unnerved the interpreter. I guess he didn't realize that all GI s didn't smoke. After another hour to two and some food, I was told that my confession was not sincere enough or long enough so I should do it again. This time I used every big word I could think of, spread the words out, increased the space between the lines and wrote the same thing. It increased the length to seven pages. After a short pause I was told to return to my hut, and I was never bothered again.

Operation Big Switch: Repatriation, August 1953

During the second week of August 1953 the International Red Cross arrived at Don's camp to assist with repatriation. Just before the Red Cross arrived, the Chinese organized the POWs into three groups. Company One had 700 troops, Company Two had 700 troops, and Company Three had 200 troops. It didn't take long for Don, who had been assigned to Company Three, to realize that the company was made up of what the Chinese called reactionaries. Don knew something was up.

When the Red Cross representatives looked over the list, they asked the Chinese why the uneven numbers. The Chinese said that they did not have transportation for Company Three, that they would follow at a later date. The Red Cross radioed Panmunjom, and orders came back that Company Three was to leave at the same time the rest of the prisoners left. The 1,600 prisoners left in trucks provided for 1,400 men. Don explained:

> We were trucked to the Yalu River and the northeast corner of North Korea to a train terminal, put on cattle cars, and rode the only restored train track from the extreme northeast corner of North Korea to Panmunjom. At the peace talks it was agreed that after a certain stage in the talks, the UN troops would not bomb this railroad right-of-way so that the Communists could rebuild it for aiding the repatriation of the prisoners.
>
> After arriving at the camp at Panmunjom, we ate pretty good. Our diet had improved vastly in the last month, since the peace talks made it look like things were going to be settled. We spent one night at their camp, and after breakfast the next morning we were loaded on trucks and moved to the area set up at Panmunjom for the exchange of prisoners. One of the articles of

Top: Overall view of Freedom Village, Munsan-Ni, where U.N. repatriated POWs were processed for return to their homes. U.S. Army photo by PFC Joe Adams, August 17, 1953. *Bottom:* North Korean women prisoners of war in Enclosure 12-F, POW Camp 1, Koje-do, burn mattresses and blankets after being notified of their impending repatriation. U.S. Army photo by Private Robert Jarocha, July 31, 1953.

The POWs inside their compound in Enclosure #2, POW Camp #1, Koje-Do. U.S. Army photo by Private Allen Johnson, August 29, 1953.

the peace agreements included a no-man's-zone of probably 500 yards that each prisoner had to walk across to prove his intent that he wanted to be repatriated. The odds were a little lopsided. Twenty-one GIs refused repatriation, and 50,000–70,000 Chinese and North Koreans refused.

After crossing the line, we were greeted by a U.S. Army general who saluted and shook our hands. Close behind the general was an American flag. I and many others broke into tears when we saw the American flag waving in the breeze. We then went into a tent and were given time to spend with a chaplain.

The next stop was a hot shower and new clothes. Then we went to bed to relax. Nurses brought us a list of foods we could have. I remember the roast beef, mashed potatoes, gravy, corn, bread and butter, milk, and apple pie à la mode. It was wonderful.

The next day my jaw started swelling. I had not used the right side of my mouth for over a year because of bad teeth. I was given penicillin for one week before the dentist pulled two badly infected teeth.

The next day we were loaded on helicopters ten at a time and were airlifted to the port of Inchon. After the 30 minute ride, we were loaded on small boats and were taken out to a troopship anchored in the harbor.

The next day we sailed for home. There were probably 200 repatriated prisoners on the ship and about 2,000-3,000 regular returning troops. We were kept on a separate deck of the ship. We were not allowed to mix with the other troops. We even had our own mess hall. We had a special diet, along with a number of pills that we had to take. The other troops were always watching us, and we had fun acting strange in front of them.

During the two-week boat ride, we kept busy being interviewed by doctors about our treatment. Because there had been a few prisoners who had refused repatriation we were all suspect of no-telling-what. Every one of us had an individual sit-down with the psychiatrist. I'm not sure, but I think I am the only one out of the 200 who didn't have to go back for three or four more sessions. I didn't have anything to hide, and I told the psychiatrist everything I knew and what I thought about it. Many of the GIs were coy and didn't open up, which the doc saw through right away. Before it was over, he told us that most would not have problems adjusting to civilian life. We had a few group sessions before it ended.

We pulled into San Francisco harbor, under the Golden Gate Bridge, · and docked at the Presidio area. It was a wonderful sight and a wonderful day. My mom and dad and other family members were waiting on the dock. We had a great time, and after a day of processing we caught a plane home.

Home: September 1953

After a week of relaxing at home, Don returned to his high school. He looked around for a while and went in to see the principal. Harry McMillian shook Don's hand, and while Don visited with others in the office, the principal left. A short time later he came and got Don and took him to the gym. Harry had called an assembly of the entire school. "Tell them that growing up is not that far away," Harry asked.

"I talked for about 40 minutes," says Don, "and basically told the kids about my POW experience. I don't know if all of them went home and told their parents what I said, but some must have because for the next six months I gave over 25 speeches to various groups all over the city."

Points of Interest

Relatively the size of Utah or Minnesota, Korea is about 2,000 years old. In that time the country has been invaded 900 times. It has had five major occupations and four major wars in the past 100 years.

—— —— ——

One marked difference between Korean POWs and all other American groups of POWs was the Communist indoctrination, or brainwashing, as it was often called. The truth is the Communists had no secret methods of brainwashing prisoners. Actually their practices are based on the simple and easily understood idea of progressively weakening an individual's physical and moral strength. The exhaustive efforts of several government agencies failed to reveal even one conclusively documented case of actual brainwashing of American prisoners of war in Korea. The 21 who decided to stay with the Communists were not sincere converts to Communism, but rather were influenced by expediency, opportunism, and fear of reprisal.

– 2 –

STAFF SERGEANT
THOMAS B. GAYLETS
U.S. ARMY

C Company, 2nd Combat Engineers, 2nd Division
Captured When the Chinese Overran His Position
Prisoner of War
May 17, 1951–September 1953
Camp One

High School Graduation: A Call to Duty, June 1950

By the time Tom Gaylets graduated from high school on June 15, 1950, he and his mother were living home alone. All of Tom's brothers had served in World War II except for one, who was currently in Korea. Tom needed work to help his mother get off welfare and decided to join the army.

After a trip to the U.S. Army recruiter in July 1950, Tom reported to Fort Knox, Kentucky, for six weeks of training. While in training Tom received a letter that told him he could be discharged because he was the only son left at home. But as Tom said, "My brother is in Korea, and he needs me." By October 1950 Tom was on his way.

Korea: The Battles, October 1950–May 17, 1951

Tom landed at Inchon, Korea, in October 1950 and was immediately assigned to C Company, 2nd Combat Engineers, 2nd Division. The unit's duties were to blow up bridges, make roads, and locate and remove enemy mines. Tom and his unit moved up and down Korea, engaging in 21 battles, in seesaw weather of 100 degrees in the summer to 40 below zero in the winter. "It was nothing but a hellhole because we fought the war 24 hours a day, seven days a week," Tom explained. "There was no such thing as going to the rear for a couple of

18

days. We stayed on the front lines all the time. We ate a lot of cold C-rations, and some days we went without eating because it was impossible to get supplies up to us. We didn't have the right clothes, weapons, or tools to do what they wanted us to do. It was just a bad situation."

The Capture: May 17, 1951

On May 16, 1951, Tom's commanding officer called him to the front lines to let him know that he would be leaving the next day at 7:00 A.M. Tom was excited. He sat in his foxhole all night thinking about his arrival back home. How happy his mom would be to see him. How proud his brothers would be that he had served. How nice it would be to have some good food and to sleep on a comfortable bed.

But the next morning at 5:00 A.M. those dreams were shattered when the Chinese troops attacked the 2nd Division and overran Tom's position. Just two hours before he was to go home to a civilized life Tom was captured and thrown into a time of dejection, humiliation, and turmoil. "We started to move north in minutes because our unit was moving up and they wanted us out of there, Tom surmised. After they got us to a holding area we stayed until night to move. We marched only at night because the Chinese wanted to hide us from our planes. The Chinese made us carry their equipment, and when we would go by one of our camps that the Chinese had just bombed they would try to get us to drive the jeeps and trucks, but we told them that we didn't know how." For the next two weeks the march was filled with sickness, hunger, and fatigue. "The Chinese didn't give us anything to eat," Tom explained. "We ate what we could find along the way. After about two weeks we marched up to the Yula River about twenty miles south of Camp One." It was a mining camp, and the weary POWs stood on shaky legs as an interpreter called out their names. Tom had given a wrong name when he was captured, and when his name was called he didn't answer. The second time his name was called, he answered, but the Chinese interpreter didn't believe him and walked over to Tom and hit him in the face with his fist. The result was a broken nose for Tom and a set of instructions to answer properly when called. The guard was nicknamed "Mule Face" after that, according to Tom, not because of the attack but because the guard actually looked like a mule. Every day in the mining camp a few men died from dysentery and starvation. "Before it was over, three-fourths of the 286 men that I had been captured with died from dysentery and starvation."

Although there were men dying all around him, Tom was faced with a desperate situation. Not only was he starving and plagued with dysentery, but he was dealing with swelling from a broken nose and knee. With no medical aid at all it was up to Tom to pull himself through this situation. Tom had a strong desire to live and to see home again. He reached deep inside and told himself that he was going to survive. He would live to see his family once again.

Telegrams dated June 4, 1951, and December 19, 1951, notifying Tom Gaylets's mother of her son's status: missing in action, and possibly a prisoner of war.

Camp One: December 1951

In December 1951 Tom and many of the other prisoners were moved to Camp One, about 20 miles north of the mining camp. The camp consisted of no barracks or fences but rather Korean huts made with a mixture of mud and straw. The floor had rocks so that the room could be heated in the winter. The rooms were ten feet by six feet, and there were ten POWs in each room. They were issued one blanket for every two prisoners. After eight months the ragged uniforms that the prisoners had been captured in were replaced with blue cotton uniforms. "We were issued sneakers, which were inadequate for the cold winters. Many of the prisoners had their feet removed as a result of severe frostbite."

Although this camp was an improvement the conditions were still terrible. "We had no showers, no sinks, no place to wash except in the streams," Tom explained.

> We were loaded with body lice and bed bugs. There was one toilet for each company. There was one light for two rooms, and it had to be turned off by 9:00 P.M. In the winter in subzero weather we could light a fire for one hour in the evening.
>
> The first food they gave us was pink and tasted terrible, but after a while they changed that. In the morning they gave us four ounces of bean milk. At noon three ounces of white rice, and in the evening three ounces of white rice. One day there was meat in the rice, and we thought that the Chinese had decided to improve our diet. The meat was delicious, and we looked forward to getting more. We found out the next day that a rat had gotten in the rice, and the Chinese had failed to take it out before serving the meal. There would be no more meat until 1953, when the Chinese occasionally started feeding us dog meat.

Deaths. During the two years Tom was in Camp One, 1,500 men died. In the winter the dead were wrapped in a sheet and dropped on the hillside. In the summer the dead were buried in a one-foot grave. Near death himself, Tom had lost 100 pounds during his captivity. Weak from bouts of dysentery, he went on burial details with shaky legs. But he kept his spirit up and made a vow to himself that he would make it.

In the Hole. The Chinese were always looking for excuses to punish the prisoners. Tom had a friend who fell out in formation every morning with an army hat on. The Chinese would put him in a four-by-four-foot hole and leave him for the day. At night they would take him out, and the next morning he would fall out with the hat on again.

Tom went to the other company area a couple of times to see friends, and the Chinese would take him into a hut, start a fire, and leave him closed up for

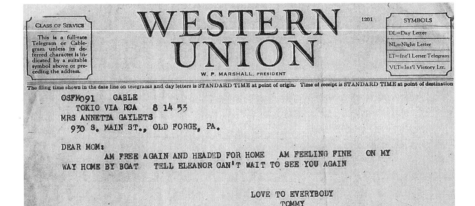

Top: Telegram announcing Tom Gaylets's imminent return. *Bottom*: Telegram from Gaylets to his mother, announcing he is on his way home.

three or four hours. "I would almost burn up in there from the heat, but they never broke my spirit or the other men's either. I think that bothered the Chinese more than anything. They couldn't figure out why we were so strong."

Repatriation: August 9, 1953

"In July 1953 a truce was signed and we knew that we were going to be released." It had been two and a half years and although Tom had had freedom on his mind from the moment he was captured, it was difficult for him to believe that that day had finally arrived.

On August 8, 1953, Tom and the rest of the prisoners were transferred to Freedom Village. Free at last, they were given showers, medical checks, new clothes, and plenty to eat. The first thing Tom asked for was a chocolate milkshake. He downed the shake, and just as soon as it hit his stomach it came back up. His body could not take the rich food. The other prisoners were in the same shape. They were sick all the way back to the States.

Welcome Home

When Tom arrived at Old Forge, Pennsylvania, he was met by a huge crowd. He couldn't believe it. They had a huge parade for him, and everyone was giving him gifts. It was a great feeling to be home. As Tom drove through the parade, he smiled and waved. He was glad to be home, but inside he couldn't help but be saddened for he had not forgotten the 1,500 men who never left the camp.

Epilogue

During the parade Tom met his future wife. They were married shortly afterward and have been married for 43 years. They have three children: Raymond, Mary, and Thomas. In addition, they are the proud grandparents of seven.

Points of Interest

On April 6, 1953, the first plan to repatriate prisoners was agreed to by the Chinese, North Korean, and American governments. Operation Little Switch was to be an "all for all" swap of the most ailing prisoners on both sides, regardless of number. On April 20 the operation began with a swap of 6,670 from the UN command side and 684 from the Communist side—a ratio of one to ten. Those returned to the Allies were 471 South Koreans, 149 Americans, 32 British, 15 Turks, and 17 other UN personnel. Authorities believe that some of the healthier prisoners were released for propaganda purposes.

—— —— ——

After the armistice was signed on July 27, the exchange of pris-oners began on August 5, 1953, and ended in September.

This operation was called Operation Big Switch. During this final exchange of prisoners, 7,862 Republic of Korea POWs, 3,597 American prisoners, 945 British POWs, 229 Turkish POWs, and 140 others were released.

– 3 –

CORPORAL
DANIEL L. JOHNSON, SR.
U.S. ARMY

1st Battalion, Company B, 38th Infantry Regiment,
2nd Infantry Division Captured at the Pusan Perimeter
Prisoner of War
May 19, 1951–August 19, 1953
Camp One

High School Graduation: A Call to Duty, July 15, 1950

Dan Johnson graduated from high school in the spring of 1950. He came from a family of seven children raised in West Virginia. There was no opportunity or much future at the time so Dan joined the U.S. Army. Dan completed nine weeks of basic training at Fort Knox, Kentucky, before being sent to Aberdeen Proving Grounds in Maryland for light artillery mechanic training. He was then sent to Japan for duty.

The 38th Infantry Regiment

The 38th Infantry Regiment was located in Fort Lewis, Washington, as part of the 2nd Division. The regiment was supervising the training and conducting summer camp when it was called to Korea. The troops arrived in Pusan in August. Their first orders were to defend the Naktong River. From late August through September 1, they repulsed attacks by the North Koreans. They took Hill G285. They lost Hill 208 and lost and regained Hill 115. In late September they retook Hill 208.

In October 1950 the regiment was responsible for the defense of Suwon-Hansong and the Yonju area close to Seoul. In late October it became part of

Task Force Indianhead, near Pyongyang. The regiment engaged in several battles throughout the months until February 1951, when it set up a defense known as the Pusan Perimeter.

The U.S. Army was being pushed south by the North Koreans at a rapid rate. Although U.S. forces had made defensive efforts, they did little to slow the well-trained advancing North Korean army. The U.S. army was at last at a point where it could no longer continue to withdraw and still maintain a foothold in Korea.

The Naktong River was the major hurdle to the NKPA (North Korean People's Army) on the Pusan Perimeter. It was the last large river for the army to cross to get to Pusan. At this line the Americans set up their last stand. It was at this time that Dan Johnson joined the 38th Regiment.

The Pusan Perimeter: February 14, 1951

The North Koreans were advancing south very rapidly. Their army proved to not be only well equipped, but also well trained. They used guerrilla warfare tactics, which were very effective. Their gunners were very accurate with their mortars. Their snipers were almost impossible to detect because they used smokeless powder. And they used high-velocity guns.

The outnumbered U.S. Army rushed troops south of each North Korean outbreak and established a roadblock in an effort to slow the North Koreans' advance. When they pushed through, a new position would be set up. This tactic did little to slow the rapid southward advance by the North Koreans.

The North Koreans stated that they would push the U.S. Army into the sea. At the port city of Pusan the U.S. Army set up the Pusan Perimeter along the Naktong River. Orders were that there would be no more withdrawals.

When Dan arrived in Korea, the Pusan Perimeter was the front line. Dan explained:

> The unit I was a member of began the push to cause the Chinese and North Koreans to return above the 38th parallel. Several delayed encounters were put in place by the enemy, each causing deaths and wounds in our unit. Our final push was in April 1951 when we were at the 38th parallel. The 38th Infantry Regiment was due for some of the men to rotate back to the States.
>
> We set up a defensive position at the 38th. We dug bunkers and had additional supplies of hand grenades, rifle grenades, and ammo. We put in minefields in front of our positions. We conducted daily patrols in front of our positions. The enemy was gradually getting closer to our position in that the patrols were making daily contact. We had a hunch that the North Koreans would mount a major offensive attack. Our hunch was right.

The Attack and Capture: May 17–19, 1951

At about 4:00 P.M. on May 16, 1951, the North Koreans made a major attack on the defensive position of the 38th Regiment. The fighting was fierce. Heavy rains set in and the defensive positions were quickly overrun. Dan, along with five other soldiers, hid on a mountainside. Dan described what happened:

> Just at the break of dawn, a small group of Chinese soldiers were searching for a pistol. The 54 others had already been captured, and a BAR [Browning automatic rifle] man had thrown away a Colt .45. He had failed to remove the holster from the belt. The Chinese were looking for the pistol and found us.
>
> We had eluded the enemy from May 17, when we were overrun, until 6:00 A.M. on May 19, when they captured us. The Chinese took us to join the other 54 already captured. Then we were taken back through our positions and minefields, and they hid us under a cliff late in the day.
>
> That night they started the march. We were marched at night and hidden during the day—outdoors. We had no medical care and no sanitation. The food was a brown powder and very little of it. This sort of condition continued until June 6, 1951, when we arrived at a mining camp. We were housed in an old building, a Japanese barrack from World War II.
>
> Many of the prisoners begin to die, some from starvation. Others died from the lack of medical care for their wounds. Everyone was plagued with dysentery, which became a cause of death for many also.
>
> After about three months at the mining camp we were marched to Changsong. The march began on September 18, 1951, and we arrived at Camp One on October 8, 1951. A short time later many of the prisoners began to die—mostly from the extreme march with no food, and then to make things worse we were bombed by U.S. B-24s. Several of the prisoners were wounded and killed during the bombing raid.

Camp One

Camp One at the village of Changsong was the second of the major camps established after Camp Five. It was located in the valley of the Yongji River approximately five miles from where it flows into an estuary of the Yalu, and less than ten miles from the Yalu River itself.

Approximately 200–300 Chinese were posted in the camp. The guards were posted in the corners of the interior of the camp with submachine guns. A few fences were erected in the camp in the summer of 1952, but at the time Dan arrived there were none. The prisoners were housed in small huts, divided into squads, enlisted men separated from officers, and blacks separated into their own compound.

An aerial view of the mountainside of Outpost #4, POW Camp #1, on Koje-Do. U.S. Army photo, April 13, 1953.

Living Conditions. The prisoners were issued a winter pair of cotton padded pajamas. The weather was brutally cold in the winter—40–50 degrees below zero—and just as hot in the summer. There were body lice, dysentery, intestinal worms, pneumonia, night blindness, beriberi, frostbite, skin disorders, dental problems, starvation, and the threat of death to contend with. There was little medical treatment and no records of it kept.

During his imprisonment Dan suffered from extreme dysentery, night blindness, and boils, and was infested with lice.

Indoctrination. Dan and the other prisoners were indoctrinated daily. The sessions lasted from morning to night, with only a short break for the Chinese to eat lunch. The prisoners usually received no food during this time. The brainwashing sessions were conducted through the time that Dan was a prisoner of war.

The prisoners had a cognitive that they were required to repeat to the Communists about what they had learned about the Communist philosophy. The guards would come into the huts at night and make Dan and the other prisoners sit facing the wall, and, with flashlights shining in their faces, repeat the cognitive. The idea was to break the prisoners' willpower down with constant harassment, lack of food, and fatigue in order to get them to convert to communism. "On one night when the temperature was -45 degrees, we were assembled outside in the snow to watch a Russian propaganda film. All of us about froze, and my feet were numb," Dan recalls. "We had to listen to a speech about how great the Communist system was and how bad the American capitalists are." The fact of the matter is that Dan and the other prisoners usually just mumbled to themselves when speaking, and the Communists were unsuccessful in their efforts to change the patriotism the U.S. prisoners of war had for their country.

Repatriation

On July 27, 1953, the armistice was signed between the Communists and the Americans. The prisoners were informed that the war was over. There would be an exchange of prisoners during a 60-day period when one-sixth of the prisoners on each side would be exchanged daily. The last of the prisoners would be exchanged on September 5, 1953.

Each day Dan waited for his name to be called and finally it was, on August 19, 1953, at Panmunjom. Dan had been a prisoner of war for 27 months. As Dan walked to freedom he thought, "I am thankful for God's compassionate care of me during this terrible ordeal."

American repatriates are issued new clothing before they are flown to Inchon. U.S. Army photo by PFC Joe Adams, August 9, 1953.

Life Afterward

A successful businessman, Dan has still had his bouts with adjustment from his experience. He has suffered from nerve problems, flashbacks, frost-bite, arthritis in his joints, and heart disease. All of these problems have occurred as a direct result of 27 months of abuse, starvation, and lack of medical care. But regardless of his problems, Dan is thankful he made it through the ordeal, is thankful for his life, and still believes in the United States of America.

Points of Interest

On June 25, 1950, when the North Korean People's Army invaded the south, it was 135,000 strong, with as many as 30,000 combat veterans from the Chinese Communist Army of World War II. In addition, the Soviet Union provided 3,000 military advisers and supplied the North with 173 tanks, 32 naval vessels, and 197 planes.

The Republic of Korea Army was approximately 98,000 strong, but only 65,000 of those were combat troops, and many of those had only finished basic training. They had no air force, no tanks, and only small anti-tank weapons, and their 11 big guns had a seven-mile range as compared with the 17-mile range of their invaders' guns. The few naval vessels they had were U.S. surplus, and those were located in Hawaii.

———   ———

According to medical experts who have studied the long-term effects of the hardships of captivity, all POWs suffer from some type of stress disorder or, at a minimum, premature aging. In comparison, one year of exposure to war ages a man by two years, whereas one year as a prisoner ages a man by four years.

– 4 –

SERGEANT
WALTER G. ADELMANN
U.S. ARMY

7th Regiment, 1st Cavalry Division
Captured After Being Wounded on Pork Chop Hill
Prisoner of War
November 6, 1951–August 13, 1953
Camp One

"What If" in His Life: 1943–1950

Walter often thinks about the "what if" in his life: what if he could have taken advantage of the tryout with the St. Louis Cardinals. At one time in his life Walter lived and breathed baseball. He was good. In 1943, at the age of 15, he was signed up to play the following season with a Cardinal farm team. Walter was a little guy, built like a catcher, and the scouts liked his hustle. Walter played Class B baseball during the 1944 season. In 1946 he played Class A baseball for a Southern League team in North Carolina. In 1947 Walter played for a White Sox farm team. In between he played with teams around his home in Joliet, Illinois. While Walter was busy with baseball, another world event was unfolding. In the summer of 1950 across the Pacific the Korean conflict had erupted. It was downplayed by politicians as a "police action" but it would turn out to be another war that would last for three years. It was an event that would change Walter's life forever, because just as he was about to try out for the St. Louis Cardinals he got a call from Uncle Sam. Walter received his draft notice.

Drafted: December 12, 1950–September 1951

Walter's turn to serve his country came on December 12, 1950, in a draft office in Chicago, Illinois. After a physical exam and a battery of written tests

Walter Adelmann as a young soldier.

Walter was drafted into the U.S. Army and sent to Fort Lenderwood, Missouri, for training. The first thing Walter faced was the frustration and anger of a lot of World War II veterans who were called back in from the reserves. Most of them had just begun to start their lives over after four years of war, only to end up back in the army.

After several weeks of drill, physical exercise, and combat training, Walter completed his basic training at Fort Lenderwood. He received orders for an old Coast Guard base, Fort Ward, in Port Townington, Washington. Many of Walter's friends were send to Fort Ward with him, and many of them were lucky enough to stay throughout the war. Walter wasn't so lucky; he received orders to Korea, along with the supply sergeant and several other fellow soldiers.

The Battle of the Hills: September 1951–November 1951

Walter arrived on Korean soil in September 1951. "When I got there I was assigned to the 1st Cavalry Division," Walter explained.

> We were sent right on the battle front, and we were on a different hill every day. The battles would later be called the battle of the hills. The unit was taking a beating. Most of the men had been wounded, killed, or captured, or were missing in action. I ended up on Hill 200, nicknamed "Pork Chop Hill," which was located by the Indian River. We would take it in the daytime and then lose it at night. One day we took it in the daytime, and there were planes coming in to get some of the men. A lieutenant was yelling and waving to take cover while he was on the radio directing planes in for a air strike. We took the hill back again. I had never seen so many Chinese bodies. There were so many bodies in the foxholes, we had to drag them out

of the foxholes in order to get in and take cover. We knew we were going to get hit that night, and we were running low on ammo. So we rounded up some of the Chinese wooden hand grenades, to use that night. We were getting hit real hard; the Chinese just kept coming. Wave after wave of them. Finally, one of the bravest men I ever knew, Sergeant Cockrun, ordered us to form a perimeter; he said, "Ya know, this looks like Custard's last stand." He still had humor in the midst of battle. The Chinese blew their bugles and started charging the hill wave after wave. I got hit in the hand and the arm with a burp gun. After we fought for most of the night we were finally overrun.

The Capture: November 1951

The Chinese recaptured the hill. All the men around Walter had been killed, and he lay among the dead American and Chinese soldiers. He had two severe wounds in his left arm. " I wiped blood on my face and played dead," Walter said.

I hoped that the next day the Americans would retake the hill. I lay there most of the day. Some Chinese soldiers ran over the top of me, but thought I was dead. My arm was badly infected and swollen badly. I decided to try and make it off the hill, but that was a mistake because the Chinese captured me. I thought that I was the only one that they captured, but they had caught some the day before, and the day before that. We had to walk for a couple of days, but finally some trucks picked us up. In addition to the fever I had developed from my wounds, I came down with anemic dysentery. I met my best friend, Jim Gallagher, on the truck. He had been captured the day before me. He wrapped me in a blanket and took care of me on the long trip to the camps. He saved my life.

The Mining Camp: November 1951

Walter and the other prisoners arrived at a temporary transit camp southeast of Pyongyang near Suan. This was one of several temporary camps; it was named "Mine Camp," or "Mining Camp," or "Soup Camp" by the American prisoners. The prisoners in these camps suffered from dysentery, severe weight loss, cold injury, tissue loss, pneumonia, and infectious hepatitis. "We were at the mining camp for about two weeks," Walter said.

The Koreans were in charge of the camp, and they were a lot rougher than the Chinese. The Koreans hated Americans. They wouldn't give us any medical treatment. Everyone was sick, and about half of the guys died that were in the mining camps. We were given a little rice to eat, but the dysentery was so bad it did little good. We had to get up and walk around to stay alive. Many of the men who came down with it died within a couple of days if they didn't keep walking around. Jim Gallagher came down with it and died a short time later. He had saved my life and now I was burying him. We had a gravesite we called Boot Hill where we buried our buddies. It was a daily task because men were dying every day.

Then Walter and many of his fellow POWs were moved to a permanent camp—Camp One.

Camp One: December 1951–August 1953

Camp One, at the village of Changsong, was the second major permanent camp established. It was located in the valley of the Yongju River approximately five miles from where it flows into an estuary of the Yalu, and less than ten miles from the Yalu River itself. Walter explained:

The camp had no fence around it, but we had guards. You could get out of the camp, but the trouble with escape was that we stuck out among the Orientals. I talked to some of the sergeants and the other POWs who attempted escape, but they didn't last long. Even in the dark the Koreans could tell the way Americans walked.

One of the first people I met was a POW who had served in World War II. He had survived the Bataan Death March and three and a half years as a POW under the Japs. When he was called back into the service he was told that he would not have to serve on the front lines. He didn't, but his outfit was overrun and that included the headquarters that was located in the rear of their position. Every time things got really bad I would think of him. Someone has always had it worse than us.

Clothing. We were issued winter clothes. They were cotton padded pajamas. "Cotton pads," we called them. They were warm and helped against the brutally cold winters of 40–50 degrees below zero. Even with the clothing there were large numbers of POWs with frostbite conditions. In the summer we would have to shed the padded clothing because the summers were just as hot as the winters were cold.

Living Conditions. The living conditions were bad. There was body lice, dysentery, intestinal worms, pneumonia, night blindness, beriberi, frostbite, skin disorders, dental problems, starvation, and the threat of death to content with. I had constant bouts with dysentery. The Chinese gave me some medicine for my dysentery and for the wounds on my arm, but neither helped much. I just kept the wound as clean as I could and that helped more than the medicine did.

I had a tremendous weight loss. I was below 100 pounds, and it seemed I was losing every day. All we had to eat for the first six months was turnips and rice. After about six months we got some potatoes, and the Chinese gave us a few fishheads. I think that is why we were having so much trouble with the dysentery. But when you are starving you will eat anything.

After the war Walter wrote a letter to the newspaper about his experience in the POW camp. It best describes the experience:

The Thoughts of a Former Prisoner of War

To be a prisoner of war is to know hunger. I am not talking about the hunger you feel when you miss your lunch or when you cannot stand your diet. I am talking about hunger from the lack of solid food for weeks and months.

Hunger that gnaws at your vital organs and strips the flesh from your bones. Hunger that forces you to eat anything and everything available...black stale bread made from sawdust, watery soup infested with worms and made from garbage, rotten potatoes and turnips dug from the muddy fields, and, if you are lucky, hot water to wash it all down.

To be a prisoner of war is to experience cold. Not the cold, blustery Minnesota winter when you wish you had worn your gloves. I am talking about standing for hours in soup lines in freezing weather pelted by sleet, feet numb and fingers nearly frozen. You are sick, your body is racked by controllable shivering and your mind is a mask of pain. Dysentery knots your stomach, adding to the misery. You begin to wonder if death is far away. It never comes. It merely teases you.

To be a prisoner of war is to experience fear. Nameless terror as you lie packed into a railroad box car, doors locked and barred, while attacking aircraft bomb and strafe and not knowing if you will be blown to bits the next second. The terrible fear of catching a horrible disease that runs rampant throughout the camp and no medicine or strength to fight back. The fear that you might never again be free.

To be a prisoner of war is to experience anger and deep depression. Anger knowing that your enemy counterparts, imprisoned in the United States, are well fed and clothed. Thoughts of family and home lock your mind in bottomless depression and is perhaps the cruelest torture. Anger at your captors and wishing for their death.

To be a prisoner of war is to suffer the agony of rehabilitation in a suddenly alien world. It is the frustration of trying to cope and fit into a society that seems foreign and unable to relate to your experiences.

It is the resentment you immediately feel for those who have never felt what you have, seen what you have, and whose personal problems pale by comparison. It is the recurring nightmares that will plague you for the rest of your days. It is the nagging question, "What was it all for? What good did it do? Who cares?"

Perhaps there was a purpose. Perhaps the POW has a clearer perspective of what is real and who is genuine. Perhaps he understands what is really important in life . . .

Indoctrination. A marked difference between the Korean prisoners of war and those in other wars was the Communist indoctrination. As Walter said,

The Chinese tried to brainwash us. They said the United States was imperialistic, run by a wealthy few and that Communism reflected the aims and desires of all the people. We had classes in the camp with the Chinese trying to get us to pick up on the Communism, but they didn't have much success. They kept going over and over the Communist doctrine. They tried to cause us not to trust one another, and for a few that worked, but they didn't make any headway there either. After a while they gave us pamphlets and books to read, but that didn't work either. We just listened to them and then concentrated on surviving the war.

Sports and the Dream. By late 1952 conditions improved in the camps. The prisoners were getting a little more to eat, and the Chinese brought in sports equipment to keep the POWs busy. They had intercamp Olympics. Walter continued to play ball in the camps, and he still had that burning desire to play Cardinal baseball. One day Walter wrote to the Cardinals: "I told them that I was a prisoner of war, but I wanted to try out for the club when I was released. They sent me a letter back and told me that as soon as I got home they would let me try out. That tryout was at the top of my priority list of things I would do when the war was over."

Repatriation: August 1953

In early August 1953 Walter and his fellow prisoners noticed that there were no planes humming overhead. The Chinese guards were acting a little different, although the POWs couldn't quite understand why. Then one morning the camp commander informed the POWs that a cease-fire agreement had been signed on July 27. "All the prisoners would be released within 60 days. We were overjoyed," Walter said. "It was like a dream." Soon after, Red Cross packages began to arrive, with soap, towels, toothbrushes, food, and cigarettes. Then, after 22 months of captivity, Walter was released on August 13, 1953.

A communist member of the joint Red Cross team, touring POW Camp #1, Koje-Do, attempts to enter a restricted area and has to be ushered out. U.S. Army photo, August 29, 1953.

Welcome Home: August 1953

Walter arrived at Lockport, Illinois, on August 31. He was met at the airport by two state police motorcycle cops who escorted him into town. The entire town showed up to welcome Walter home as he was paraded down the center of town in an open convertible. The Lockport mayor gave him the key to the city. Walter was glad to be home, and his parents were glad too. His mother noticed that Walter seemed nervous, but shrugged it off, considering all that had happened to him. The nervous condition would prove to be more serious than that. Walter wouldn't be able to forget about the battlefields and all of his friends who were buried on Boot Hill.

When I got out of there my dad had a new car agency. I told a lot of my friends, who wanted to come and get a car off me. Several of my buddies came with their backpay and bought cars. I made quite a bit of money, and then I got $5,000 in backpay from the army. I ended up going to Havana, Cuba, with one of my friends. We went down to Miami first, and the weather was terrible, so we flew over to Havana, and I started drinking pretty heavy. The alcohol really got hold of me. I drank for two months solid. I was trying to forget Korea.

Walter Adelmann displays his two Purple Hearts.

Battle Fatigue

When I returned home I checked into the Veterans Hospital. They told me I was suffering from battle fatigue. I stayed there for a while and was released. My drinking problems continued. I never tried out for the baseball team. I just continued to drink until 1962. I went to Alcoholics Anonymous then, and I turned my life over to a higher power, and I went to those meetings and it helped me. I don't think I would be here today if I were still on alcohol.

Over the years Walter worked as an ironworker for the Tennessee Valley Authority, got married, and raised six children.

Epilogue

I'm staying with one of my daughters. We have five daughters and a son; he's 27 years old—he was the baby. It took me five daughters; I was trying to get a baseball player. To get lined up with the Cardinals, maybe make it like I didn't do. We used to pack 'em in when we played in those days. It was nothing to have 7,000 people watching you play a baseball game.

I still haven't received the Purple Heart for my wounds. I'm in for it now; Congressman Harry Walder said he's going to get it for me. When I got out, I received letters stating that they needed more information. I get 40 percent disability for my nerves and for being a prisoner of war. I didn't get anything on the hand and arm, so they didn't have a record of that.

As I look back on it, fighting on Pork Chop Hill made me proud to be an American. To see some of the regular army in action, to remember when we formed the last perimeter before the Chinese final attack, and to hear in the middle of battle someone who still had humor—"Ya know, this looks like Custard's last stand." It makes me proud. You know something else, I have never stopped being a Cardinal fan."

Forty-five Years Later

In January 1998, Walter sent a letter and a newspaper article. He had made the headlines in his local newspaper as a war hero—rightfully so, because in

September 1997, after 45 years of having no medals to prove that he had been in battle, he received six combat medals for his service in Korea: two Purple Hearts, the National Defense Service Medal, the Korean Service Medal, with four battle stars, the POW Medal, and the United Nations Service Medal.

– 5 –

1ST LIEUTENANT
WILLIAM H. FUNCHESS
U.S. ARMY

B and C Companies, 19th Infantry, 24th Regiment
Captured During the Battle of Anju
Prisoner of War
November 4, 1950–September 6, 1953
Death Valley, Camp Two, and Camp Five

Clemson College: ROTC, a Call to Duty, 1948–1950

Bill's first experience with the military was in the Reserve Officers Training Corps (ROTC). During this training Bill was uniformed, marched to meals, and had inspections, and he woke each morning to the tune of reveille and went to sleep with the tune of taps.

Students were being drafted daily, and Bill had difficulty keeping up with the number of his friends who had been inducted. When Bill's number came up, he went to Fort Jackson for preinduction but was deferred until he graduated in 1948. At that time Bill was commissioned as a 2nd lieutenant in the U.S. Army.

A few months later Bill was sent to Fort Jackson as a training officer for new recruits. A rumor was floating around in early 1950 that the fort was going to be closed, and Bill was transferred to the 19th Infantry in Japan.

On June 25, 1950, Bill's unit received news that the North Koreans had invaded the South, and a week later, on July 4, 1950, the short-handed 24th Infantry Regiment boarded four LSDs and headed for Korea.

The unit was ill equipped, with a few small tanks, some corroded hand grenades, old vehicles, and weapons left from World War II. To make things worse, support from South Korea would be next to none. They had made no preparations to fight a war.

Kum River: The First Combat in Korea, July 1950

The 24th Regiment landed at Pusan, Korea, one day after they left Japan. Bill's battalion set up a defensive position where the main road crossed the Kum River north of Taejon. The unit was transported by train, and Bill's platoon of fewer than 50 men dug in on a half-mile section of the dike that ran parallel to the river.

The first night was uneventful. The next day the unit recovered small-arms ammunition from an overturned South Korean truck. The engineers blew up a bridge, and Bill had his photo taken with his platoon sergeant, O. J. Mixon.

That night Bill heard a rumbling sound and realized that it was enemy tanks across the river. The tanks stopped at the blown bridge, turned right, and lined up directly across from Bill's position. They opened fire, but did very little damage. However, the tank attack was followed by a mortar attack, which was more effective. Several of the rounds landed in the foxholes, causing casualties.

The next morning the tanks headed for a train tunnel to hide from the planes. The bombing raid was ineffective, and for the next several days Bill's unit was attacked by the tanks.

Enemy troops had gotten behind Bill's unit. Bill and his unit had become isolated on the dike. With a half a box of World War II grenades, Bill and his men fought their way out, reaching a road totally exhausted. Just when they thought they were safe, they ran into more enemy tanks.

The unit was overrun, and Bill decided to play dead. That only lasted for a few minutes because Bill saw the North Koreans bayoneting wounded soldiers. Bill crawled into a ditch.

A tank came by and turned toward Bill. He had no place to go except on top of the tank. Suddenly he heard someone shouting that he wasn't a gook, but rather a GI. It was one of his own tanks. Bill scrabbled inside and crouched on the floor until the tank was a half mile away from the battle. Bill had narrowly escaped death.

Lieutenant William H. Funchess.

Pusan Perimeter

The North Koreans continued to advance. They claimed they would push the U.S. Army into the sea, and their better-trained and equipped forces were well on their way to accomplishing what they said they would do. The U.S. Army continued to be pushed south.

The tactic of the Americans was to rush soldiers south of each North Korean unit to slow down the advance. Finally, Bill's unit stopped at the port city of Pusan, and orders were that there would be no more withdrawals. The Pusan Perimeter was set and the fighting continued. The fighting was intense. Each battle had a story. "One dark night we were dug in but were being attacked," Bill recalled.

Funchess (on phone) is pictured here with Sergeant O.J. Mixon.

There was a lull in the fighting and all was quiet. While in my foxhole, I began to get a whiff of a strange odor. The smell got stronger, and I heard something no more than ten feet away. I realized the odor I was smelling was a North Korean soldier who had been eating garlic. I shouted, "Halt," and was answered with a burst of fire from a burp gun.

I fired back, and then a North Korean patrol dashed across the crest of the hill into a mine field we had set. Several were killed, and one who spoke English was wounded. He kept calling out, "Don shoot, I GI!" The next morning we captured the wounded North Korean soldier.

The fighting continued, and the North Koreans did penetrate the perimeter, but they were never successful in pushing the U.S. Army into the sea.

Charging North: Taejon, Anak, Bob Hope at Pyongyang, Anju

Suddenly many units begin to pour into Korea, along with supplies and equipment. On September 15, 1950, the Inchon Invasion was launched, described

Corporal Howard Moll, Captain Louis Rockwerk and Funchess march through Taejon.

by some historians as the boldest military maneuver in history. Bill was still at the Pusan perimeter, but he couldn't hear the battle and artillery in the distance. The battle destroyed North Korea's ability to fight a successful war.

Within a few days Bill and his unit returned to Taejon, where just two months before they had been forced out by the North Koreans. The civilians were glad to see the American troops and provided apples, wine, and flowers. The soldiers stayed in Taejon for several days, waiting for supply trucks to catch up. While waiting, Bill and several of his men returned to Kum River. It was hard to recognize the area, but they were surprised to find out that a soldier from Company C had been hiding in the mountains since July 16.

Bill returned to Taejon and received orders to go into the mountains to look for North Korean guerrilla units. They were successful in capturing some North Koreans, but for the most part the North Koreans had disappeared.

Bill's unit departed Taejon and continued the march north. They stopped at Kaesong just south of the 38th parallel. They didn't know if they were going north, but by afternoon they received orders to continue the march. Just before arriving at Anak, which was located between the Yellow Sea and a large mountain range, the U.S. soldiers heard gunfire. They found out that the non–Communist civilians had taken over the city for the Americans. It was North Koreans against North Koreans, and little did the Americans know of the atrocities that day.

The Americans continued north with little resistance. After a couple of days, Bill's unit reached Pyongyang, the capital of North Korea. After watching Bob Hope and Marilyn Monroe in one of their shows, the 24th Regiment continued north. The North Korean villagers seemed friendly enough: They clapped, smiled, and seemed to be happy, but the 12 South Korean soldiers with Bill's unit sensed that all wasn't well. They kept talking to the North Koreans as they moved and learned that there had been Chinese troops seen in the area. Continuing north, Bill and his men were on edge as they closed within 20 miles of the Chinese border.

Suddenly the U.S. soldiers received orders to stop their advance and begin an immediate withdrawal. They found out that heavily armed troops were massing to the rear of their position. The withdrawal began, and the units were picked up by trucks and moved to Anju, where they set up a defensive position.

A short time after taking position, Bill's unit spotted Chinese troops by the thousands advancing across the river and reading straight toward their position. Bill's unit and several of the other units began firing on the Chinese. The Chinese took cover and became more conservative with their advance. They had been slowed, but Bill knew it was only temporary. There were simply too many of them.

The Capture: November 4, 1950

Suddenly I felt a sharp pain in my right foot, and I realized I had been hit. I stumbled, and Lt. Mike Dowe and a GI grabbed me. The GI took my carbine, and then the two of them began pulling me up the mountain. At the time I became extremely thirsty but knew there was no time for a drink of water. I turned my head to look behind and saw only dead or wounded GIs on the ground. The Communist machine gun crew had done its job. A few surviving GIs were climbing the mountain about 40 yards to our rear.

The surviving GI slung my carbine over his shoulder, and then he and Lt. Dowe got on each side of me and began helping me up the mountain. I was holding on to both of them as we struggled up the mountain. Suddenly the GI was hit by small-arms fire, and he fell down the mountainside.

We took a few more steps, then rested for a minute beside some trees. At that time Lt. Dowe assured me he was going to help me walk and would not leave me to fend for myself. He was true to his word as he tugged, pulled, and pushed me toward the top of the mountain.

Mike and I were going through a stand of saplings when all of a sudden, a Communist soldier appeared no more than a dozen steps away. He immediately let go with a volley of rounds from his burp gun, and I saw bark flying from the trees in front. Luckily, neither of us was hit. I saw a dumbfounded expression on the Communist soldier's face, as he was no doubt wondering why we didn't fall. By the time we could get a few rounds off with Lt. Dowe's carbine, the soldier had disappeared. We didn't bother checking to see if we had killed him.

We reached the top of the mountain and went down the other side. We were walking across a narrow valley and suddenly came to a large ravine we had not seen before. It must have been 20 feet wide and 50 or 60 feet deep.

As Lt. Dowe and I were trying to figure out how to get across the ravine, we suddenly heard a loud commotion, on both sides of us. We looked and saw 40 or 50 Communist soldiers, no more than 50 yards away. They were shouting at us, but we could not understand what they were saying. They began moving toward us in somewhat crouched positions and had their rifles and burp guns trained on us.

Lieutenant Dowe and I held a hasty conference to decide our next move. We would be killed if we jumped into the ravine. The steep mountain was behind us, and armed soldiers were on both sides with their weapons trained on us. We realized the situation was hopeless, so we threw the carbine into the ravine since we were out of ammunition. We watched helplessly as the enemy soldiers closed in with every rifle and burp gun trained on us.

As the Communist soldiers got nearer, they motioned for us to raise our hands. We reluctantly complied. It was the most helpless feeling.

The soldiers stood in a semicircle around us, each with his weapon trained on Lieutenant Dowe or me. They were still yelling, and I saw anger on their faces. At that time I realized our captors wore uniforms that were not familiar to us. I suspected that they were probably Chinese, although I had been assured by my superiors earlier in the day that no Chinese forces were in North Korea. My suspicions were later confirmed, as those were indeed Chinese troops. They turned out to be seasoned soldiers who had been engaged in China's recently fought civil war.

Suddenly a small Chinese soldier, scarcely five feet tall, burst through the crowd. He wore the same cotton padded uniform as the others, except he had on fur-lined leather boots. He walked within inches of me, stopped, reached up, and pulled my right arm down and started shaking my hand. Then he spoke in perfect English: "We are not mad at you. We are mad at Wall Street."

I was dumbfounded. I didn't know what they meant. I was confused, not to mention scared stiff. I was also relieved that Lieutenant Dowe and I were not killed on the spot. It was November 4, 1950. China had entered the war, and apparently one of their missions that day was to take prisoners. I asked the interpreter what his nationality was. He hesitated and finally answered with two words: North Korean. I knew he was lying.

Bill and other prisoners were tied with communications wire and marched off into the ravine. They experienced several hits in the back and legs with rifle butts, but considered themselves lucky when they witnessed a number of their soldiers bayoneted when they were too weak from wounds to walk.

The prisoners had stopped just about an hour before sundown. Bill noticed that his foot was swollen and removed his boot. His sock was filled with blood, and Bill realized that the bullet had done considerable damage to his foot.

Suddenly reality set in, and Bill realized that many of his platoon had been killed or wounded. He was shivering from the bitter cold. He was scared, confused, and angry.

"As darkness approached, we were rounded up and forced to march to a small North Korean schoolhouse about a mile away." Bill recalled.

Pain flashed through my foot and leg with every step. GIs from my platoon assisted me in walking to the schoolhouse.

We were hastily searched as we entered the dark, unheated building. I managed to hide my compass and pocket Bible in the sock on my left foot. Escape was uppermost in my mind, and I planned to make a run for it as soon as the opportunity presented itself.

More captured U.S. personnel were thrown into the school building. It was dark. I would quietly ask each group to identify themselves. Most were from C Company, but some came from the weapons platoon. All were scared but hoped to be rescued soon.

Sleep was impossible for me because of the pain in my foot, the crowded conditions, the silent plans for escape, and the cold that was tearing through my body. Little did I realize the worst was yet to come.

A jeep pulled up in front of the schoolhouse, and the angry Communist doctor got out of the jeep. We learned that he had been strafed by American planes and he was quite upset. We thought the doctor had come to treat the wounded American soldiers. But we were mistaken. He applied bandages to all of the wounded Communists and deliberately avoided even looking in our direction. Finally, in desperation, I walked up to him, lifted my bloody foot and pointed to it. The doctor looked away and continued working with the wounded enemy soldiers. I finally got the doctor's attention after several more attempts. He gave me a disgusted look and then pointed to a bloody bandage on the ground he had just removed from a wounded enemy infantryman. It was as if he were saying, "You can have the bloody bandage; you can take it or leave it."

As I stood there dumbfounded, he turned away again. I picked up the bloody bandage and wrapped it around my foot as I knew I had to stop the bleeding. I never gave a second thought to the possibility of contracting a blood-transmitted disease.

The March North

Just as the march north began, the weather turned nasty. The temperature dropped below zero and it began to snow. Bill had just begun the march when one of the Chinese guards grabbed the collar of his field jacket and began pulling. A few steps later Bill was walking in subzero weather without a field jacket.

The prisoners had walked only a short distance when they came to the Chongchon River. They were ordered to strip and swim across. On the other side, Bill stepped out of the river and shook the water off as best he could. He had one positive thing happen: he noticed that the bandage was gone from his wounded foot and that the bullet had caused a large gash in his foot but had not gone through his foot. It was much easier for Bill to handle psychologically.

Bill put on his clothes and one boot, and one of the men piggybacked him. The guards were yelling and threatening the prisoners with bayonets. They were in a hurry. Bill said: "The next morning U.S. planes strafed us, and the attack lasted for about ten minutes. We were angry because they didn't realize that they were attacking their own troops, and the Chinese were angry because the attack happened at all. Luckily no one was injured."

The guards gave Bill two empty bags and a couple of poles to make the makeshift stretcher. For a couple of days men from C Company carried Bill, but after that Bill told the men to go on, that he would make it on his own.

He was left with two guards who were jabbering between themselves. Bill was the topic, and he knew he was a burden and would probably be shot. While the guards were jabbering, Bill noticed that the makeshift stretcher had one pole that was larger on one end and only about five feet long. He crawled to it, picked it up, and made a crutch out of it. He started down the road, and the guards followed.

After a while, one of the guards started double-timing and caught up with the main group, while Bill was left alone. Bill hurried as fast as he could, but the guard showed no mercy. He yelled and threatened Bill with a bayonet.

As daylight approached, the prisoners spent the day hiding in the valley. When nightfall approached, the weary prisoners stood on shaky legs and began the march again. Bill was in a semiconscious state when he felt someone pulling on his finger. He turned, opened his eyes, and saw an enemy soldier pulling at his wedding band. When the soldier saw that Bill's eyes were open, he began yelling something, and so Bill removed the ring and gave it to him. He hurried off as if he didn't want the other guards to know he had taken the wedding band.

The POWs marched all night and hid the next day. Then, just before darkness on the third day of the march, the Chinese brought out the first food the prisoners were to be given. It was two buckets of corn. It had been shelled from the cob and soaked in water. The prisoners were told to put some in their pockets because the march would be long.

As the march began Bill's hands and feet became numb. He stumbled and fell. He crawled to his feet at the sound of yelling guards, only to walk another 100 yards or so and fall again—never, though, did he give up.

On November 8, four days after Bill's capture, he celebrated his twenty-third birthday. He spent the day in a crowded room, and they had a meal that day. It was boiled millet seed. It tasted awful, but it was food. Lt. Mike Dowe wiggled near Bill and wished him a happy birthday.

The Chinese noticed that the prisoners were getting weak and gave them a pep talk. The Chinese soldier told the prisoners that just over the next mountain they were going to get milk, honey, bread, and cheese at the prison camp. The prisoners were never to see any of it.

The march continued for three weeks. Bill had bruises from falling, his wound wasn't getting any better, and on occasion he and the other prisoners were paraded before North Korean villagers as the prize stock of the Chinese. Extreme hunger pain plagued the prisoners, but the thirst was even greater.

On November 18, after a hard night's march, some Chinese officials showed up. After going over the POWs, they selected four GIs, and Bill and the others found out the four prisoners were being turned loose. It was a propaganda move on the part of the Communists. It paid off because the release hit the headlines.

Bill's wife read the articles and immediately wrote to the four released POWs. They let Sybil, Bill's wife, know that he had been wounded in the foot at the time of his capture on November 4. They never saw him again.

Finally, after four weeks of marching, the prisoners reached an isolated, snow-covered valley about six or seven miles north of Pyoktong. There were several mud huts with thatched roofs. Bill and the others were housed inside. It was to be their home for the next eight weeks. They called it "the Valley," for lack of a better name.

Death Valley

Bill was placed in a mud hut with 12 other wounded soldiers. His hut was called the sickhouse. "My shack was constructed with cakey walls about four inches thick," Bill said. "A roof of rice straw, a sliding door covered with rice paper, one small window, also covered with rice paper, and a mud floor. The room was nine feet square, and the walls were about four and one-half feet high on the front and back of the shack. The only place I could stand without bumping my head was in the center of the room. There were no closets and no furniture, just four walls. Neither was there any provision for light. There was an open three-foot porch outside the door."

After a day or so, the Chinese begin feeding the prisoners twice a day. The diets consisted of partially cooked grain in a single bowl. All the prisoners took turns getting their food with their hands. Then small bowls were issued. The bowls were about the size of teaspoons. No meat or vegetables were ever given with this starvation diet.

The toilets were primitive—they were nonexistent. The prisoners went outside, but the odor was not bad because the cold temperatures immediately froze anything. Inside, however, the smell of infected wounds from pus and decaying flesh was sickening.

The valley was a nightmare. "Inside the room in the valley were the most downcast men I had ever seen." Bill stated:

All of us had been wounded, some seriously. All of us would have quickly recovered if we had received just basic medical attention. But there were no drugs or painkillers. There were no bandages to keep open wounds covered. I kept complaining to the guards, but they always angrily muttered something in Chinese and abruptly turned away. I didn't know what they were saying, but assumed that if translated it would mean something like, "The hell with you."

The wounded men tried to be brave, but I would hear sobbing at night. They often asked how long it would be before the U.S. Army would come to set them free. There were screams when the wounds became too painful to bear. There were nightmares when they slept.

There was one young GI in the shack named Hernandez who had frostbite on his fingers. The temperature in the room was so cold that his fingers became swollen and turned brown. In the early stages his fingers looked like well-cooked wieners. His fingers later turned black and the flesh began to drop off. Exposed bone extended from the end of several fingers.

The nightmare continued day after day with a new addition of body lice. They would crawl and bite. The prisoners would pop them with their fingernails. They were impossible to get rid of. They hatched in the seams of the clothes. The heat from the body helped the hatching of the eggs.

One morning in January 1951, the Chinese guards called all of us outside. We were going to be moved. In several feet of snow we began the journey. It was a march of about 20 miles. We were being moved to Camp Five at Pyoktong.

Camp Five

"I was running a high fever when we arrived in Pyoktong," Bill said.

The pain in my injured foot was secondary to the aches and pains through my body. I was completely exhausted, nauseous, had diarrhea, and just felt like I would be better off dead than alive. The next morning when I woke, I knew some type of sickness had come over me but didn't know what it was. I just wanted to rest and then sleep some more. I had no energy, and when I stood I became dizzy.

The first meal in Pyoktong was more of the same, a cupful of boiled seed. It tasted awful.

I asked the GIs about the officers. They told me the officers were isolated several hundred yards away. For just a second, I wondered why I was not with them, and then I lay down on the floor and fell asleep.

After a while, I looked around and saw I was in a mud shack similar to those in the Valley. The rooms were perhaps a foot larger in each direction, but they still had mud walls, mud floors, and paper on the doors and windows. The room I was in also had a narrow closet, which extended along one wall. I could tell we were again being housed in a shack that was previously occupied by a Korean family.

After a while I went outside the room and saw dozens of other mud buildings similar to the one I was in. Some had straw roofs, while others were covered with clay tiles. The Chinese had taken over that residential area, put a barbed-wire fence around it, and called it a POW camp. They said it was Camp Five.

As I looked toward the west, I saw a large body of water, which I later learned was a manmade reservoir on the Yalu River. Somebody told me that China was just beyond the farthest inlet. Suddenly a strange feeling came over me when I realized we were so close to Red China. I was afraid I might be taken into China while I was in captivity.

There was an inlet north of our camp, a lot of houses to the south, and the officers' compound on the east. The town was beyond the officers' compound.

I saw a lot of building that had been burned. There was a shell of a concrete building facing toward the officers' compound which I later learned was a glass factory. In the distance, I could see the steel doors of a destroyed building. Nothing else remained. There were empty foundations scattered around. There was a lot of burned tin that came off the roofs of some industrial buildings.

The Chinese had lied to us again. They told us they had built a POW camp, but I saw nothing they had constructed except the fence. Even the meals were the same.

A couple of days after Bill arrived, a Catholic priest appeared in the camp. He was carrying a pan that was fashioned from a piece of rusty tin. He was from the officers' compound, and Bill wondered how he got into the camp.

Some of them told Bill that he was Father Emil Kapaun from the 1st Cavalry Division. Bill watched as he scrounged a few cornstalks, several small scraps of wood, and some corncobs. He set up a few stones, built a small fire, and then filled his pan with snow. As the snow melted, he added more, and finally he had a pan of warm water. Then Father Kapaun offered each of the prisoners about one-third of a cupful. It tasted so good. It was the first or second day of February and this was the first time Bill had had a drink of water since his capture on November 4.

GIs were beginning to die from freezing and starvation. The dead were thrown outside. It was a horrible sight. The bodies were covered with blood, body waste, and snow. It was a dreadful scene.

I had been living in the compound with the GIs for about a week when, all of a sudden, an English-speaking Chinese soldier appeared at the door. He asked me my name and then wanted to know my rank. I was sure he already knew the answer to both questions. He then told me to follow him, as he was taking me to the officers' compound.

The Officers' Compound. Bill felt weak and drained. When he arrived at the officers' compound, he was met by a doctor, also a POW, who immediately saw that Bill was sick. He looked at Bill's fingernails, pulled up his eyelids, and then informed him that he had hepatitis. Everyone was getting it.

Death became a serious problem. "We couldn't figure out why some died, but we knew some died from starvation and some from pneumonia," Bill explained.

We always wondered who would be next. Death usually came quickly. A man could appear to be healthy and then dead within a week. It was scary.

On one occasion I was in a room with Lt. Dick Haugan and some officers I didn't know. Dick was from Van Nuys, California, and was our company executive officer. He has been hit in the left foot by rifle fire while I was hit in the right foot by machine gun fire. Dick recovered from his wound before I recovered from mine, so I gave him my left boot. That gave him a pair. I didn't need boots anyway because there wasn't much walking I could do with hepatitis.

It wasn't long before Dick got sick. The army doctors in the camp diagnosed his problem: pneumonia. He got weaker and weaker and quit eating. His throat had a rattling sound as he slept.

One night in early 1951 I was asleep on the mud floor between Lieutenant Haugan and an officer from another division. If I ever knew his name, I don't remember it. The next morning, when it was time for our usual cup of millet seed, I tried to wake the officer on my right, but he was dead. Then I turned and shook Dick. Blood gushed from his mouth and he was dead too.

That struck me like a blow between the eyes. I couldn't believe that men on both sides of me had died during the night and I didn't even know until the next morning. Two men out of a dozen in one night was frightening.

Would I be the next to die? Several times I said that aloud to the others in the room as we lay down for the night.

I became so sick I couldn't eat. My company commander, Capt. Louis Rockwert, would lay my head in his lap and feed me like a baby. He did so for several days. Then I began to have hunger pains. I felt that was a good sign, that I was getting better, but hunger pains were almost unbearable.

Stacks of Bodies. One day while he was outside, Bill was shocked at the number of deaths that were occurring. "I saw piles of bodies," Bill said.

They were stacked like cordwood. The stacks were three or four feet high and often 30 or 40 yards long. There were usually several such stacks. The bodies were emaciated and often partially covered with snow. Closer inspection revealed that the clothes were ragged and covered with blood and body waste. Some had their eyes open while others were closed. However, all had a look of agony etched on their lifeless faces.

It was more than I could stand. Here were the bodies of America's finest young men frozen, covered with filth, and lying in stacks in a hostile country.

The deaths were needless and should have never happened. But we were among fighting people, Chinese and North Koreans, who hated us with a passion. Just a little medical attention, a few pieces of warm clothes or blankets, and some decent food would have saved those men. We complained to our captors, but it did no good.

A Record of the Dead. One of the men from the 1st Cavalry Division managed to get into camp with a camera loaded with film. Walt Mayo, a young lieutenant from Boston, asked me to go up in a nearby bombed-out glass factory so we could photograph the next burial detail. He wanted to use the photos eventually to help prove the large number of deaths that took place in Camp Five.

Walt and I climbed up on the second floor. He took up a vantage location while I kept an eye out for the guards. He got some good shots as the POWs carried frozen bodies on their shoulders, two men to each body. There must have been several hundred dead that cold winter day. We watched as they let the camp and placed the bodies in the snow near the reservoir. Since the ground was frozen, there was no way to dig a hole for burial.

Dog tags were collected from the dead so that they could be turned over to the proper authorities after the war ended. The Chinese guards would have none of that, however, and they confiscated the tags. Some of the men on that burial detail said they left the second tag in the mouths of the victims, but the Chinese took those too. For some reason the Communists were deliberately trying to destroy the identities of the dead.

Walt used the camera to make a spectacular shot of a sick officer. We didn't know what his ailment was, but his testicles had enlarged to the size of grapefruit. They were so heavy that they hung down to his knees. I am sure the photo would have been of interest to our U.S. authorities and medical personnel.

It proved difficult to keep a secret in the POW camp. Some way or other, the Chinese guards learned about the camera and confiscated it. Needless to say, the Communists made it mighty rough on Walt, but he never implicated me.

I kept thinking about a way to hide a list of the dead. It then occurred to me that I might be able to hide a list, if I wrote small enough, in the blot-

CAPT WAYNE BURROUS 28/7/51
LT. WAYNE K. BURROWS ?/2/51
L/COL CLARK G. CAMPBELL 8/5/51
LT. ULYSSES BRADFORD 21/1/51
LT. HOWARD O. CALDWELL 16/5/51
CAPT. RODNEY F. CLOUTMAN ?/2/51
MAJ BART N. COERS 1/4/51
CAPT. NORRIS L. COLEMAN 11/4/51
W.O. JOSEPH LACKNER 7/7/51
MAJ. FRED D. CHESTNUT 15/7/51
MAJ. JESS E. EVENS 20/3/51
MAJ. OSCAR E. ESPELIN 13/2/51
CAPT. ALEXANDER DIDUR 19/8/51
LT. ALBERT G. FRENTZICH 3/3/51
LT. CHARLES GILL
W.O. ENOS E. FALLS ?/8/51
LT. FRED GIROUX ?/4/51
LT. JOHN D. GRIEVE ?/3/51
LT. PHILLIP K. GLENN 16/4/51
LT. ALLAN HENSLEE 25/4/51
MAJ. HOMER C. HINCKLEY 23/5/51
CAPT. HELGE E. PEARSON 3/5/51
CAPT. KENNETH HYSLOPP 10/12/50
LT. ? R. HARRIS ?/2/51
CAPT. DURFEE LARSON 21/3/51
MAJ. E.J MURPHY 11/6/51
LT. ALFRED RASKIN 9/2/51
LT. DEWITT SMITH ?/?/51
LT. JAMES SULLIVAN ?/3/51
W.O. JAMES E. STEPHENS 14/5/51
LT. ROLAND V. SUND 5/7/51
LT. GRANT SIMPSON 9/7/51
SGT. RUSSEL WOODARD ?/4/51
MAJ. FRED W. WINTER 12/7/51
CAPT. FRANK M. WHITE 15/1/51
CAPT. WALKER ?/1/51
BOB ENGLEHART., SGT. McALLISTER
SGT. GEO. E SCHOONOVER ?/3/51
SGT. ROBT. L. MAYS
PFC JESSE L. MITCHELL
LT. RICHARD HAUGEN 7/3/51
7321/OSTROM AVE., VAN NUYS, CAL.
CPL. RAYMOND STRATS ?/12/50
M/SGT. F.J. McDONALD
LT. GEO. BULKOWSKI 11/6/51
LT. W? E. BIVENS ?/3/51
MAJ. ARNOLD N. BRANDI 19/5/51
LT. FRANK S. JOHNSTON 20/2/51

MAJ. WILLIAM O. WILSON A.F
W.O. ADOLPHUS NAVA 1/3/51
CAPT. RONAL L. HARRY A-F
CAPT JOHN PAYTON A-F
CAPT JAMES ALDER A.F
LT. VICTOR MAGEE INF
LT. PAUL TURNER A.F.
ENS. DALE FALER NAVY
LT. J.T. WITT AF. CAF
CPL JAMES MACHANEY (MECH ANTY)
CPL. ROBERT FESTA (FENTA) AF
ENS. ROLLO BUSCH N.
F/LT. TREYOR FNYER. S. AF. AF
CAPT. JOSEPH LISTON CAN. AF
CAPT. PHILLIP GREVILLE-AUS A.F.
LT. RALPH OLWETTE INF.
CAPT. ROBERT MADDEN AF
LT. ROBERT NEVILLE AF
CAPT. PATRICK FLYNN MAR. AF.
CAPT. ROBERT ? MAR. AF.
CAPT. JOSEPH KUTZS (KUTYS)
LT. ROLAND McDANIEL MAR INF.
CPL. JAMES KIERMAN? AF.
CAPT. ROBT.C. HENRY (HARRY)? AF
CAPT KENNETH P. LERRER AF
SGT. LE HEUSEUX OR ?
OR L. HEUSEUX A.F.
M/SGT. CARRELL HODGES AF
SGT. FRED PARKER AF
M/SGT JAMES (CAIN)(CARN) M-AF.
ENS. HARLO STERRETT NAVY
CAPT GERALD KUBICEK (KUBINEK)
CAPT. SAM BAUGH A.F. AF
CPL. MANLEY AF
LT. SYDNEY KANNER AF
ENS. JOHN DE MASTER N-AF.
LT. CHARLES J. SMITH
MAJ. BUCKY HARRIS M-AF.
CAPT. ERUL J. KAPAUN 23/5/51
LT. THOMAS KILBY 30/5/51
LT. WILLIAM KELLUM 11/7/51
LT. JACK W. LEADBETTER 5/3/51
MAJ. GEOFFERY LAVELL 7/3/51
CAPT ROLAND KUBINEK 15/7/51
LT. EDMUND McCULLOUGH 7/3/51
LT. CHARLES MAYRAND 20/7/51
W.O. LEO J. MANEGREE 6/3/51

List of POWs rolled inside a fountain pen and smuggled out of Camp #2, Pin-Chon-Ni, by Lieutenant Funchess. Originally believed to bear only the names of deceased POWs, the list is now known to include survivors.

ter of my fountain pen. I borrowed short lists provided by the other POWs and consolidated them. There was no way to verify the accuracy of the lists as POWs were constantly being taken to the sick house or transferred to other compounds. I rolled up the list and hid it in the fountain pen.

Indoctrination. Some POWs in Camp Five thought they were probably the first U.S. military personnel to be subjected to the Communist version of political indoctrination. The Americans called it brainwashing. "The lecturers began early in the morning and continued until noon," Bill recalled.

They took about a 30-minute break so the Chinese could eat. They gave us no food while they ate. Then the Chinese would start again and continue until nearly dark. They gave it to us first in Chinese and then it was translated to English. That made it doubly boring.

By the time that we finished our cup of millet seed at night, the Chinese would come into our rooms with flashlights. They made us sit on the floor with our backs to the wall. Then they would go around the room and demand that each POW give his cognition of the subject being discussed. We resisted, but the Chinese were very demanding. If we refused to answer, we were in big trouble. Most of the time when our turn came to give our cognition we just rambled in our conversation without really saying much about the subject. That satisfied the Chinese in most instances because we had not openly defied them.

There was one period when the brainwashing subject was writing by some Communist leader. They went on and on with the contents of the writing until we wanted to throw up.

When it came time for Major Hume to give his cognition of writing, he said, "It's not worth the paper it is written on and the paper is not worth a damn." The major was thrown in a small structure partially underground near one compound. It was loosely constructed and may have been used as a chicken house at one time. A guard was always nearby to prevent other POWs from communicating with the major.

The weather was harsh, and it was doubtful whether the major had any warm clothing or blankets. I am not aware of the guards ever letting him outside to go to the bathroom. If not, he was living with his own body waste.

It wasn't long before the end came. The major died as a direct result of the barbaric treatment by the Chinese Communists who controlled Camp Five. Major Hume's death was an atrocity committed by the Chinese and was most certainly a war crime.

The major's death in Camp Five was deliberately planned and carried out as an example to other POWs. It certainly had a sobering effect on me. It proved to us that the Communists, indeed, were most serious in the conduct of their indoctrination.

Starvation, Hunger Pains, Stealing Food, and Malnutrition. The diet for the prisoners in Camp Five was nothing more than a starvation diet. Millet seed was the usual food, but they did get cracked corn and dried soybeans on occasion. This was portioned in a cup full twice a day. The major cause of death for 60–70 percent of the prisoners was the lack of food.

The Chinese cooks were misfits from the Chinese Army. They had no sanitary practices, and they weren't smart.

POWs began cooking, and the taste of the food improved. The guards would ration out the grain for two or three days at a time and do so carefully so that the prisoners didn't get too much at one time. On one occasion, when two prisoners died, the Chinese guards returned to the kitchen and took back the portions of the two dead prisoners.

Bill got his first meat four months after he was captured. It was March 15, 1952. The prisoners had received a couple boxes of fatback and pork livers. The cooks chopped it up very fine and put it in with the millet seed. The prisoners could taste the meat, but there wasn't a piece large enough to chew on.

"Several months later we got some more meat," Bill recalled.

That time it was dried fish, which arrived from China in wooden boxes. When we opened the boxes there were more maggots than fish. As hungry as we were, it turned our stomachs, and we threw fish, boxes, and all on the trash pile.

Later on that day the guards came around and wanted to know how we prepared the fish. The cook on duty told them the fish was full of maggots and it was thrown away. That angered the Chinese, who stated emphatically that the fish would be eaten and not discarded.

The cooks went out to the trash pile and retrieved the fish. They put the fish and maggots in bags and doused them several times in pots of hot water. Then they threw bags, fish, and maggots away when the Chinese weren't looking. Then the guards stood around the eating area to make sure that we ate our fish soup. It was all I could do to keep from throwing up when I realized I had eaten cooked maggots.

The hunger pains were terrible, and the starvation drove the prisoners to do things that they would never have considered if they had been well fed. It made them take chances with their lives. They would risk death for pieces of meat. Several times Bill and others would sneak into the kitchen and storage areas and steal food. On the one hand it helped them stay alive, and on the other it would have cost them their lives had they been caught.

The malnutrition took its toll. Bill and many of the others suffered from beriberi. The corners of Bill's mouth were split, and it felt as if the skin on his tongue was peeling. He suffered from night blindness and weighed less than 100 pounds.

The First Message from Home. After his capture Bill had never received or sent any letters. His family didn't know whether he was alive or dead. One day the Chinese guards announced that they had a tape recorder and that any POW interested could tape a 60-second message. Some of the messages would be broadcast over the radio, but they made no promises.

Bill took advantage of the opportunity and knew that if the message was to get out he would have to lie. He sent the following message:

Dear Mom and Dad,

     Am a prisoner of war in Korea. Am fine. Don't worry. In warm build-
ing. Clothing good. Hope you got my last letter before capture. Give my love
to Alice. Nanny. Hope to see you all soon. Tell Dad to look after the farm.
Hope to get home soon. Hope to be home and we have no more wars.
                                        Sincerely,
                                        Love Always, William

Bill's message arrived in late April or early May, just before Bill's father passed
away. That was the first word that anyone received concerning Bill's status. In
later years it gave Bill satisfaction to know that his father had learned he was
alive prior to his own death.

     First Haircut. None of the men in Camp Five had been given haircuts
since their capture. Bill's hair was driving him crazy, and his beard had become
a nesting place for lice. Often he would borrow fingernail clippers to trim the
hair around his mouth. "One day the Chinese brought an old Korean farmer
into the camp," Bill explained.

     He had a pair of shears with two long handles. We were told the old
     farmer would cut hair with the shears. The farmer worked fast, spending
     only a minute or two on each POW. When it came my turn, I sat on the edge
     of the little porch to my shack, and he started on my head working the two
     handles as fast as he could. The shears were dull and pulled my hair a lot. I
     asked him to clip my beard, but he didn't understand me. He finally caught
     on to what I wanted and clipped my face, leaving stubble about one-fourth
     inch long; however, it really felt better.

     Mail Call. By the end of 1951 the prisoners started getting letters from
home. They had also been allowed to write some home. However, they had no
idea how many of them ever reached their destinations. The POWs found out
later that some were getting out. Bill figured that there were many people reading letters before they were mailed, looking for secret codes. "I fooled the Communists at least one time," Bill recalls.

     In a letter to my mother I mentioned several family members and in the
     middle of the paragraph inserted a sentence to the effect that I really wished
     I could enjoy one of Jack and Belle's good meals. The Communists didn't
     know that Jack and Belle were the two farm dogs and that all they ate were
     scrapings of leftovers, nothing to brag about. After my return home mother
     mentioned that letter to me and said she knew exactly what I meant when I
     mentioned Jack and Belle.

POW with a Camera. The Communists were masters in the use of propaganda. They decided to provide Frank Noel, a captured Associated Press correspondent, with a camera and film. A special guard was assigned to him, and he took photos. Some of the first pictures were of POWs swimming in the reservoir near Pyoktong.

"The Chinese had held what they called Summer Olympics. The purpose of course was to spread [the impression of] good treatment of POWs," Bill said.

Moving Again

One chilly morning in September 1951, Bill and the other prisoners were called outside. There was a major search of the area. The Chinese never found anything, and the POWs never found out what they were looking for. A couple of hours later the men set out on a march. They were being moved again. After several miles a small village with about 50 mud shacks appeared. The most significant landmark was a white schoolhouse on the south end of town. There was a large valley beyond the river which extended perhaps a mile before it disappeared into the mountains. It would be their new POW camp.

Camp Two at Pin-Chon-Ni

The new camp was called the officers' camp because it held mostly officers from the U.S. Army, U.S. Navy, U.S. Marine Corps, and U.S. Air Force. Also, some British, Australian, South African, Filipino, and Turkish officers were being held in this camp.

The POWs were herded into the schoolhouse. The building faced south and had about ten rooms, each approximately 20 feet by 28 feet. On the west end of the schoolhouse there was a large room that was set up as a library containing Communist publications, books, and newspapers. Later on, there were large photos of Communist leaders placed on the walls. The room was also used for indoctrination during bad weather.

There was a long hallway on the south side of the building which extended from one end to the other. The front entrance was in the center of the building, and the main back entrance was on the opposite side. There were also entrances on each end of the halls. A nonworking latrine was in the back. There were also several small buildings behind the schoolhouse, plus several shacks on the hillside behind the school building.

The entire compound was a couple of acres in size and was surrounded by a barbed-wire fence eight feet high. The wooden posts were about 12 feet apart, with seven strands of barbed wire. Saplings, each about one inch or slightly larger in diameter, were woven vertically between the strands of barbed wire. The distance between the saplings was one and a half to two inches.

Initially there was only a single fence around the compound, but a second fence about 12 inches away was later installed. That meant that escaping POWs would have to go through two fences to get outside. Guard shacks and also a cook house were located on the east side of the compound. That building was made of mud, with a rice straw roof. It had a poorly constructed washroom on one end. A shallow ditch about two feet wide ran through the corner of the compound just beyond the washroom. That is where the prisoners got water for cooking and drinking. The Chinese guards told the prisoners the water was not sanitary. That fact was very evident when a prisoner found roundworms in a bucket used for dipping.

About 12 feet in front of the schoolhouse was a slope that extended down ten feet to a rather large level area. That is where roll call formations were held. The area was also used to play games.

Inside the schoolhouse building there was no furniture of any kind, no beds or cots, and no heat. Several months later the Chinese guards made wood-burning heaters from 30-gallon drums and placed one in the hall outside each room. They installed a stovepipe and ran it overhead horizontally through each room and then outside the wall on the south side of the building. There was limited wood to burn and inadequate amounts during the subzero winter months.

One luxury in the camp was a light bulb on the end of a drop cord. The guards controlled the main light switch and turned all the lights out an hour or two after sundown. The prisoners had to sleep on the floor, but this time on wooden floors. Eventually the prisoners would receive some thin bamboo mats which had received many years of use by the schoolchildren. Each man had a mat about two feet wide and nearly six feet long.

The rooms had wainscoting on one side about 30 inches high. The wall was hollow behind the wainscoting and served as a nesting area for large wharf rats and roaches. Sometimes at night prisoners would hear the rats running over their bodies as they slept. During the day, rats could be heard behind the wainscoting. There was no way to control the roaches. They were everywhere. There was also an abundance of flies and mosquitoes.

Camp Commander. General Deng was the new camp commander. He had fought the Japanese and then the Chinese Nationalists. He was tough. Deng always rebuked or threatened the POWs. He never said anything pleasant and never smiled. He had a deep hatred of Americans. On one occasion Deng stated, "You Americans give us any trouble, we will kill you and bury you in a hole 40 feet deep so that you don't stink up Korea."

Attempted Escapes. Escape was uppermost in the POWs' minds. Several men in Camp Two tried to escape, but none were successful. Some groups would be gone for four or five days, others for weeks before the Chinese would bring them back to camp. They were bruised from the beatings.

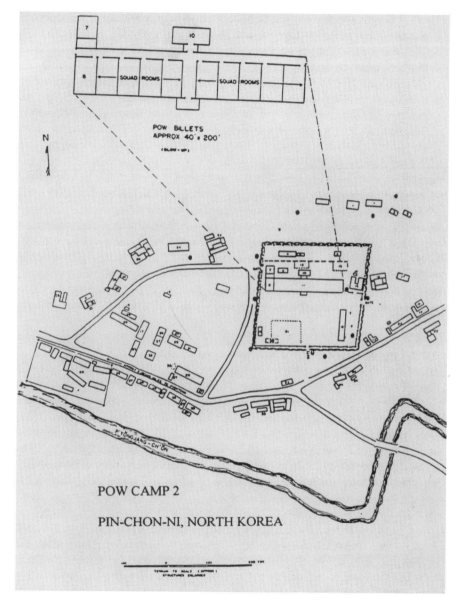

A diagram of POW Camp #2, Pin-Chon-Ni, with enlargement of POW billets.

General Deng bragged about the impossibility of escape. He felt so confident that all escapes would fail that he made each POW an offer. Each POW who wanted to escape could sign up. The Chinese would pack them a lunch and give them two hours' head start. "I don't know how many others signed up, but I did," Bill said.

I forgot about my night blindness and my injured foot. I wanted to go and foolishly assumed Deng would live up to his word. He didn't. Almost immediately I was taken out of camp for interrogation. The Chinese demanded to know why I wanted to escape. They expounded on their so-called lenient policy toward POWs. They accused me of being a warmonger and of not being sincere. The way they ranted and raved one would have thought I had committed some terrible act. All I did was take old beady-eyed Deng up on his promise. He reneged on his deal.

The Agony of POW Life. Although the living quarters in Camp Two were an improvement over those in Camp Five, the agony of life as a POW didn't change. In the winter temperatures dropped well below zero, and the prisoners were without adequate heat or clothes. Hunger pains were as commonplace for the prisoners as the sun coming up each morning. Interrogations continued; mail was used as a weapon against the prisoners and by early 1953 was stopped altogether. The war wasn't going well for the Chinese, and supply lines were cut off. This meant shortages of supplies for the Chinese, but also for the POWs. A diet of grain-sorghum was supplied and was responsible for an outbreak of diarrhea. It was just another bout with daily life as a prisoner of war.

News of Bill's Father's Death. One of the lieutenants in Bill's company escaped capture in 1950, but was captured in 1951 and showed up in the camp. Prior to his capture, his wife had corresponded with Bill's wife. She told Bill's wife that Bill's father had passed away in May 1951. The lieutenant was reluctant to tell Bill, but decided to take him aside and break the news. "The news of my father's death hit me hard," Bill said. "Tears came to my eyes, but I did not grieve for long because the misery of daily life as a POW didn't give me much opportunity to dwell on the loss of my father. I often wondered how much my missing in action played in his death at 51. I wondered if he got the news that I was alive in a POW camp."

Thirteen Days in the Hole: October 1952. "On October 4, 1952, the guards became upset with us and pulled the light switch shortly after darkness as punishment," Bill recalls.

That angered the POWs, who proceeded to make hellish racket in the rooms. It was a childish reaction, true, but it was the only way we could fight back.

POWs in the rooms yelled, whistled, banged on eating utensils, and stomped their feet on the wooden floor.

At the height of the commotion, someone came in from a trip to the latrine and said, "Funchess, there's a big Carolina moon outside."

I went outside the back door and stood there gazing up at the moon. I remember wondering if my wife, Sybil, in South Carolina would be looking at the same moon in 12 or 15 hours.

Instantly a bright light from a flashlight was shining in my face. I recognized the sound of the guard's voice as he shouted, "Come with!"

The guards began to manhandle me. I was shoved back and forth between two small groups for a few minutes. One used his fist to hit me. I realized I was dealing with an angry bunch of Chinese guards, and I became concerned for my safety.

I was thrown into a latrine, and the door was slammed shut. It was the smallest latrine I had ever seen. It would have measured no more than three feet in length and 18 inches in width. The only floor was something that felt in the darkness like two small logs with about a six-inch space between them.

I was hurt, so I tried to sit down. I sat on one log and realized I was sitting on fecal matter. But what could I do? I leaned against one wall and braced my knees against the other. I tried to wedge myself so that my feet wouldn't slip through the opening between the two logs; I knew that was down below. Before I fell asleep, the guards threw the door open. They shouted something at me and physically pulled me out of the latrine. Apparently none of the guards spoke a word of English. They led me down a dirt road and stopped near a small toolshed that had mud walls.

I wasn't so lucky as to get thrown into the toolshed. Instead, I was thrown into a hole in the ground adjacent to the shed. As I fell to the floor of the hole, I realized chickens had been the last occupants. The stuff on the dirt floor was slippery and smelled really bad, but not as bad as the latrine I had just left. The stuff was chicken shit.

For the next 13 days, Bill was not pulled from the hole, in spite of severe diarrhea, and interrogated. He was forced to write and sign a confession, and then finally on the thirteenth day he was released and sent back to his compound.

The War Ends

Some time in 1953 some Red Cross parcels arrived in camp. It was the first contact since the capture of the prisoners. The POWs received some basic toilet articles but no food. They knew then that the war must be close to an end.

Shortly after the Red Cross parcels were distributed, the POWs were assembled and told that the war was over. The prisoners were told that there would be a 60-day exchange, with each side releasing one-sixth of its prisoners daily. The final batch would be released on September 5, 1953.

Chinese army trucks arrived on the dirt road outside the compound's main gate the following day. The POWs boarded the trucks and traveled a winding road that ran parallel to the Yalu River, which divided Korea and China. After about 100 miles the POWs boarded boxcars and after a long ride arrived at a Communist holding area.

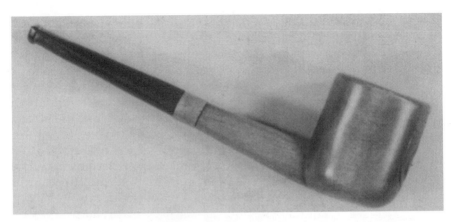

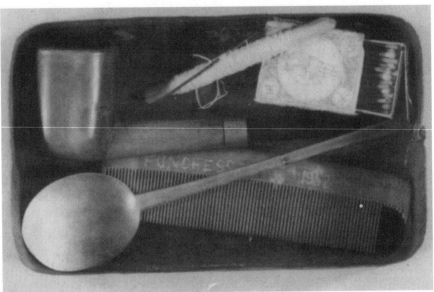

Top: **A pipe carved for Funchess by Lieutenant Art Wagner from firewood found in POW Camp #2.** *Bottom:* **Possessions of Lieutenant Funchess in a black box.**

The Holding Area: A Release, September 1953

Finally we reached the Communist-controlled holding area for POWs. It was several miles north of Panmunjom, and when atmospheric conditions were favorable, I could hear U.S. helicopters in the distance.

Some of us were housed in tents, while others were in buildings. Surprisingly, our food was not good. We received soybeans, but I soon grew tired of them. For some reason, I expected much better meals since the time for repatriation was near.

Each day the numbers of POWs were read out by the Chinese authorities. Those men were loaded on trucks for the short ride to Panmunjom. We wished them well and waved goodbye.

I secretly envied the departing POWs and hoped my name would be called the next day. Each day, however, I was disappointed.

Finally, September 5 arrived. That was the day we were told the POW exchange would be completed. A list of names was read, but mine was not included. There were also several dozen officers whose names had not been called. I became concerned and approached one of the Chinese officers who spoke English. I said to him, "I thought the POW exchange was supposed to be completed today."

The Chinese officer responded, "That's right. It's over."

Startled, I responded, "It can't be over. Why am I still here?"

"You are not a POW!" he snapped.

"What am I if I am not a POW?" I asked.

"You are a war criminal!" he shouted.

I was shocked, then asked, "What did I do to become a war criminal?"

"Remember Anak!" the Chinese officer screamed as he turned and walked away.

Anak was the North Korean city that had experienced a civil uprising as my unit approached it prior to my capture. Atrocities were committed by its citizens against one another. Nearly two years later, during a brainwashing session, those atrocities were portrayed by the Chinese as having been committed by the U.S. Army. I stood during the session and accused the presiding Chinese officer of lying and also shouted that I was there in Anak. I was taken out of the POW compound where a number of high-ranking Communist officers debated my fate while I was outside the building standing at attention. The decision that day, although unknown to me, apparently was to accuse me at the appropriate time of being a war criminal.

I was quite concerned, on September 5, 1953, I tossed and tumbled all night. I considered trying to escape to friendly lines, which seemed such a short distance away. I realized I would never get through the thousands of enemy troops and gave up the idea.

The next day an English-speaking Chinese officer separated me from the few remaining POWs and ordered me to get on the back of a waiting truck. I thought it was strange that I was the only POW on the truck. The Chinese officer then got on and sat across from me. There was an armed guard sitting beside the driver. The officer gave the signal to the driver to pull out of the holding area.

The truck drove off. I never said anything to the Chinese officer sitting across from me. The truck moved slowly and did not seem to be headed toward Panmunjom. Instead, the driver seemed to be going in circles. The officer shouted to the driver several times, but I did not know what was being said.

Funchess and his wife, Sybil, embrace at Columbia Airport after a three-year separation.

Finally the truck stopped outside a compound surrounded by a fence. About 20 young POWs approached the truck and told me they were going to refuse repatriation. One of them suggested that I get off the truck and join them. I emphatically shouted, "No way!"

I told them they were American servicemen and were expected to return home. They laughed and began taunting me. I told them they were making a mistake and said no more. The truck pulled away.

The truck moved slowly, and I had the feeling the Chinese were deliberately killing time. After a while the truck stopped in a wilderness area. The terrain was hilly and covered with trees and brush.

The English-speaking Chinese officer said, "Get off!"

I picked up my few possessions and slid off the back of the truck. I just stood there as I wondered what was going to happen. The Chinese officer shouted. "Walk down the path! If you step off the path, you will be killed!"

I saw just a narrow foot path leading into the wilderness, so I hesitated. When I hesitated, the Chinese screamed, "Move!"

As I cautiously stepped on the path and began walking, I expected a rifle shot in the back. I held my arms in front of my body in order to make as small a target as possible. But there was no rifle shot. There was only an eerie silence behind me as I cautiously walked down the narrow, crooked path. I heard the truck drive away, and I realized I was alone.

While I was walking down the path, I wondered if I was free or if I was still a POW. Nobody was in sight, and it was a strange feeling, indeed, to be alone in the wilderness. I walked several hundred yards and was careful not to step off the path. I figured it was probably mined on both sides. I realized I was walking in No-man's-land. It was a bizarre feeling.

Suddenly, in the distance I saw a U.S. Army ambulance parked where the path widened. The back doors were open, and I saw two men in uniform standing at the rear of the vehicle. They were looking down the path as if they were expecting me.

I recognized one of the men as a major, so I saluted. He said, "Lieutenant, you don't know how lucky you are to be here."

I answered, "Yes, but what happened?"

The major told me both sides had been holding war criminals. "Last night," he said, "both sides agreed to release war criminals."

My eyes became moist as I realized I was free. My war, the forgotten war, finally came to an end on September 6, 1953.

The pain and misery I suffered at the hands of my Communist captors ended after 1,038 days of torment.

Homeward Bound

Bill boarded ship and headed for the United States. It took three weeks to get to San Francisco.

As we approached the docks of San Francisco, I could hear the band playing "California, Here I Come." Wives and family members of many POWs were present, but I had asked Sybil not to come to San Francisco.

We were taken to the airport where I waited for a plane to Columbia, South Carolina. A large crowd was gathered at the gate when my plane landed at the Columbia airport. I looked out the window and spotted Sybil. She was decked out in a bright red dress so I could be sure to see her. I stepped off the plane. I was finally home.

After two months at home, Bill checked into the hospital at Fort Jackson for an operation on his foot.

On January 20, 1954, the day after I was released from the hospital, I was separated from military service.

It was time to begin a new life.

Points of Interest

Ex–POWs have a common condition called KZ syndrome. This condition is marked by such symptoms as failing memory, difficulty in concentration, nervousness, irritability, restlessness, fatigue, traumatic dreams, headaches, depression, moodiness, loss of initiative, a feeling of insufficiency, and shunning large crowds and social activities.

— — —

Of those POWs who survived the Korean prison camps 138 were considered for awards for valorous and meritorious conduct while a prisoner of war. Of those, 55 were decorated. The publicity they received was nothing compared with the misconduct trials held for POWs.

– 6 –

CAPTAIN
HENRY HUMPHRIES OSBORNE
U.S. NAVY

Squadron VF 63, CVA Philippine Sea
Captured After Being Shot Down in North Korea
Prisoner of War
May 23, 1951–September 1953
Camp Two and Camp Three

World War II: Patriotism, May 1942

In May 1942 World War II was in full swing. There was a need for fighting men, and 18-year-old patriotic Henry H. Osborne walked into a recruiting office in Dallas, Texas, and volunteered to fight for his country.

Henry signed up to become an aviator and, after passing a battery of tests, was sent to the University of Georgia in Athens for preflight school. After successfully completing preflight school, he was sent back to Dallas for Naval Aviation School. After again successfully completing this phase of training, Henry was sent to Corpus Christi for one last phase of training.

When Henry completed his training, he was sent to the South Pacific to several different carriers where he flew combat missions until the war ended. He returned to Corpus Christi after the war and was assigned as a flight instructor. A few months later he was sent to Cory, Florida, near Pensacola, before finally being sent to Georgia Tech University to complete his college education.

The Korean War: Squadron VF 63, August 1950

On June 25, 1950, the North Koreans crossed the 38th parallel and invaded the South. The well-trained Communist army outnumbered and was better equipped than that of the South Koreans. In short order the South Korean army was in retreat. The United Nations forces became involved in the effort to stop the Communist aggression, and by late June American armed forces were on their way to South Korea.

Henry was on his way to Korea in August 1950 with squadron VF 63 aboard the USS *Coral Sea*. For the next three months he conducted air raids over North and South Korea. The North Koreans were stopped at Pusan, and the UN forces began a push north. When the North Koreans were pushed across the 38th parallel it seemed that the war would soon come to an end.

The squadron, now aboard the USS *Boxer*, returned to the United States. The unit was home only a short time when the Chinese entered the war and pushed the UN troops back across the 38th parallel. The air group now aboard the USS *Valley Forge* was on its way back to Korea on December 6, 1950.

The squadron was back on the forward area on January 31, 1951. It transferred to the USS *Philippine Sea* in March 1951.

For the next several months Henry and the rest of the squadron conducted air raids over North and South Korea. Henry was due to return to the United States in June 1951. By now it was May, and he was counting the days. On May 23, 1951, Henry was leading a group of three planes over North Korea. He was lost from the group, shot down eight miles east of Singye in North Korea, and he became a prisoner of war, an experience that would last a lifetime.

The Capture: May 23, 1951

I bailed out and as soon as I landed I gathered up my parachute and headed for a ditch. I was being shot at all the time. I had a sidearm and started firing back. I didn't see any planes coming to rescue me so I held off the enemy as long as I could. I was firing and suddenly I turned and from the corner of my eye I could see a young Chinese soldier, maybe 13 or 14 years old pointing a rifle at my head. By now I had several bullet holes in my flight jacket, and I was caught hands down. I raised my hands and surrendered.

The March: Interrogation

Henry was marched for days. During the journey he was taken to several interrogation sites. At each site there was intense questioning, threats by the interrogators for lack of cooperation, and beatings. Each ended with a continued march farther north into Communist territory, the prisoners' hands bound behind their backs with communications wire. They walked at night and stopped at daybreak to stay out of the sight of U.S. airplanes.

Along the way Henry and the other prisoners were given little food. Small portions of rice and millet seed were the meals, but on some days there was no food at all. When prisoners died along the way they were left on the trail. They saw several prisoners who had been mutilated—bodies burned and castrated.

Finally, after endless days and nights of hell, Henry arrived at Camp Three.

Camp Three

Camp Three was located on the banks of an estuary of the Yalu about six miles from the river itself. The camp was divided into two sections by barbed wire. The prisoners were guarded by about 250 Chinese guards.

"I saw many prisoners die and helped bury many," Henry recalled. "Lots of the young soldiers just gave up or did not know how to take care of themselves. I saw one soldier with sores all over his body. His hair was matted to his head. I told him he better clean himself up, wash his hair, and drink only boiled water." Henry recalls the young soldier's reply: "I don't have a comb." Henry told him he didn't either, but "there is plenty of water and this is my comb," he said, holding his hand out with fingers spread.

Henry spent his first few weeks in Camp Three, and then one day he was told to pack. He and several other prisoners were going to be transferred. He didn't know where, but he was soon to find out. He was going to Camp Two. This camp held airmen, senior officers, doctors, senior sergeants, and men who the Communists felt could not be brainwashed. Henry Osborne was one of those prisoners.

Camp Two

In Camp Two I was held in a schoolhouse. This camp was composed of airmen, senior noncommissioned officers and pilots, doctors, and senior officers. The Communists wanted the older, more experienced officers segregated from the more naive, less experienced enlisted men and junior officers. They felt they could exert more influence over the younger group if they were away from the others. There were about 200 men in the camp. They had about five doctors, graduates of Oxford, Georgia Tech, West Point, Annapolis, and other universities. Some of their interrogators were just as well educated. The doctors' medical care was good, except the doctors had few supplies or medicines.

Camp Two was north, near the Yalu River. It got very cold in the winter. Our planes hit the Chosin Reservoir and thus eliminated electricity to the camp for some time. The food was barely enough to sustain living. For the 200 plus, we received rations of about one small pig a week, along with very small portions of rice and sugar. I got down to 125 pounds from the 190-pound weight I had when I was captured. I had several bouts of dysentery. I lost my voice for months at a time. The vitamin deficiency caused ailments such as beriberi and scurvy.

We had frostbite. We had to march for miles to gather firewood, and then when we brought it back the Chinese would take it and tell us that this wood was for them and that if we wanted any firewood we could return for it. We planted gardens, but often the Chinese would take the fruits of our labor.

One night there was a group of us sitting around talking. It was very cold. The group was international, and as we were talking we began to wonder how cold it was. Finally someone realized that the Europeans were talking about Celsius, the Americans were talking about Fahrenheit, and the Brits were talking about degrees of frost. Well, we decided that was no problem. It took us a long time to figure it out. We realized from the episode how dull we had let our brains get. We were being starved and spent so much time saying no in response to the indoctrination that we had turned our brains off. We realized we needed to do something and started classes teaching other prisoners: the Hispanics taught Spanish; I taught math. We had no texts and were not supposed to congregate.

Then every opportunity we had we confused our captors. We held "crazy week" and pulled pranks on the Chinese. Another camp did the same thing at the same time so the Communists thought we were communicating with another camp; we were not.

Indoctrination. There was much questioning on a one-on-one basis. The questioning went on for hours. There were Koreans, Chinese, and Russians involved in the indoctrination. I was put in solitary confinement sometimes for not being cooperative or able to learn the teachings of the Communists. When I was first captured, I was told I could write home if I would write what I was told to write—that the United States should stop its imperialist suppression of the Democratic People of Korea. My wife was six months pregnant, and I was concerned about her well-being. I wanted to write and let her know I was alive, but I could not make myself be dictated to by the Communists. I didn't expect to get back alive, but if I did I wanted to be able to hold my head high and not be a traitor. Consequently, it was five months after I was shot down before I got to write home. My first letter arrived home in October 1951. The address read: Lt. Henry Osborne, POW Camp #3, 0/0 Chinese People's Committee for World Peace, Peking, China.

One of my friends, Tom Harrison, was an officer in the Air Force. When he bailed out his leg was amputated. The Chinese, before tending to his wounds, questioned him for hours. He would pass out, and they would revive him and start questioning him again. He always responded, "My name is Major Tom Harrison, serial number," etc. They then put a bucket over his head and pounded on it. They placed a rag over his face and dripped water until he passed out. This went on for three days. Finally, they told him that he deserved to be a major and respected him for holding out. They had no use for collaborators. They used them and then deserted them. The prisoners wouldn't associate with the collaborators, and many of them just died.

Mind Games in Reverse. Capt. Johnny Thorton, USN, was a helicopter pilot and was always playing tricks. He rode an imaginary motorcycle around camp. The Chinese finally hauled him in and told him they were confiscating his motorcycle. He protested, but they insisted. He had to give up his imaginary motorcycle for a while, but it wasn't long before he had another one.

Repatriation: July 27–September 1953

The armistice was signed on July 27, 1953, and the release of prisoners started about a week later. Officially Operation Big Switch began on August 5, 1953, and ended a month later on September 5, 1953. After suffering from malnutrition, a weight loss of 65 pounds, dysentery, beriberi, scurvy, and frostbite to both hands and feet, Henry finally had hope of seeing his wife and family again.

He was one of the last to be released. He passed through Freedom Village and was greeted by U.S. officers. Henry was deloused, showered, given a medical examination, and all he wanted to eat.

PFC William Bolkcom, Corporal Leland Slavens, Corporal Stefano Salerno and an unidentified soldier, recently repatriated POWs, catch up on their mail. U.S. Army photo by Private Gwin, August 14, 1953.

Turkish repatriates at Freedom Village kiss their national flag. U.S. Army photo by PFC Joe Adams, August 7, 1953.

He came home by ship and was again examined, interrogated by military authorities, and sent to the naval hospital at Corpus Christi, Texas. After a short stay in the hospital he was released.

Flight Instructor

Corpus Christi was the hometown of Muriel Osborne, Henry's wife since 1947. Luckily for them Henry was assigned as a flight instructor. He needed to get in flight time and checked out in jets. His tour was interrupted with a tour to Monterey for six months, and then he returned to Corpus Christi.

For the next several years Henry was assigned to several bases, sometimes to fly various planes and sometimes as commanding officer of a squadron. His final assignment was in New Orleans, where by now he had been promoted to the rank of captain. After 31 years of service, he retired there as a commanding officer in 1973 and returned to Texas.

Return to Korea

Years later a group of former POWs returned to Korea at the invitation of the Korean Veterans Association. This was the first time Henry had been to South Korea. Henry and his wife were both impressed with the progressiveness of the South Koreans. They were getting ready for the Olympics.

The Osbornes visited one square in Seoul where there were hundreds of pictures of dislocated people. The square was filled with people looking for lost relatives. When the North Koreans flooded South Korea they took many hostages back with them, and many have not been seen since. The security was very tight because the visit took place shortly after the Russians had shot down a Korean plane, and recently a South Korean diplomat had been murdered while on a trip to a foreign country.

The Osbornes visited one of the tunnels that the North Koreans had dug under the 38th parallel. It was wide enough to drive a truck through. They had dug many such tunnels. As Henry looked on he thought, "They seem determined to invade again."

A Note of Success

Henry taught math to a number of the POWs while they were in prison camp. One day, after returning to the States, Henry got a call. It was from one of the sergeants to whom he had taught fractions. Of course in prison camp there were no textbooks, so it came strictly from Henry's knowledge of the subject. The sergeant had not finished high school at the time Henry taught him the fractions he needed. When he got back to the States, he took a college entrance exam and passed. He called Henry, thrilled that he had met the math requirements to enter college. There was one other thing: he had yet to see a textbook.

A Point of Interest

After repatriation operations were concluded, the UN Command listed 944 POWs missing and presumably in enemy hands. Through the efforts of the Allies this number was reduced to 470. In 1954 and 1955, American pilots released by the Chinese and the Soviets claimed that other POWs were being held. One eyewitness reported American POWs working in labor camps in Siberia. The Russians and Chinese denied the claim. After the fall of the Soviet Union, a joint commission of Americans and Russians was formed to investigate claims that U.S. Korean War prisoners of war were transferred and held by the Russians.

In 1993 the commission completed its study. In part, these were its conclusions:

1. U.S. Korean War POWs were transferred to the Soviet Union and never repatriated.

2. This transfer was a highly secret MGB program approved by the inner circle of the Stalinist dictatorship.

3. The rationale for taking prisoners to the USSR was to exploit and counter U.S. technologies and for general intelligence purposes.

4. Prisoners were moved by various modes of transportation. Large shipments moved through Manchouli and Pos Yet.

5. POW transfers also included thousands of South Koreans, a fact confirmed by the Soviet general officer, Kan San Kho, who served as the deputy chief of the North Korean MVD.

6. The most highly sought after U.S. POWs for exploitation were the F-86 pilots and others knowledgeable of new technologies.

7. Living U.S. witnesses have testified that captured U.S. pilots were, on occasion, taken directly to Soviet-staffed interrogation centers. A former Chinese officer stated that he turned U.S. pilot POWs directly over to the Soviets as a matter of policy.

8. Missing F-86 pilots, whose captivity was never acknowledged by the Communists in Korea, were identified in recent interviews with former Soviet intelligence officers who had served in Korea. Captured F-86 aircraft were taken to at least three Moscow aircraft bureaus for exploitation. Pilots accompanied the aircraft to enrich and accelerate the exploitation process.

Korean War: June 25, 1950–July 27, 1953

Country	Dead	Wounded/MIA	Total
Australia	265	1,387	1,652
Belgium	97	355	452
Canada	309	1,235	1,544
Colombia	140	517	657
Ethiopia	120	536	656
France	288	836	1,124
Greece	169	545	714
Netherlands	111	593	704
New Zealand	31	78	109
Philippines	92	356	448
ROK	415,004	428,568	843,572
South Africa	20	16	36
Thailand	114	799	913
Turkey	717	2,413	3,130
United Kingdom	670	2,692	3,362
United States	54,246	106,978	61,224
Totals	472,393	547,904	1,020,297
North Korean army			620,000
Chinese army			900,000
Total Communists killed, wounded and MIA			1,520,000

– 7 –

CORPORAL
BILLY N. GADDY
U.S. ARMY

A Company, 9th Infantry Regiment, 2nd Division
Captured During an Ambush While Laying Telephone Wire
Prisoner of War
October 3, 1951–August 29, 1953
Camp Three

Basic Training, Korea: The Front Lines, February 1951

Bill Gaddy enlisted in the U.S. Army on February 19, 1951. After several weeks of basic training at Camp Carson, Colorado, Bill found himself with a set of orders to Korea in July 1951. The next thing he knew he was sitting on the front lines at Heartbreak Ridge.

Heartbreak Ridge: September 13, 1951

The most costly of all the ridge battles fought in the fall of 1951 was that of Heartbreak Ridge. The ridge pointed daggerlike into the NKPA front lines. Taking the ridge would allow the Americans to control a roadnet now in Communist hands.

Billy's unit, the 2nd Division, was chosen to take the ridge. The 23rd Regiment was to be the assault unit and would approach the ridge from the Sataeri Valley on the east. Two battalions were to take hills 851, 931, and 894.

On September 13 the assault started, with units coming under fire almost immediately. The units moved forward slowly under constant attack. At noon

75

the 2nd Battalion crossed the line of departure and immediately came under automatic weapons fire. Two American units were pinned down while the North Koreans bombarded their positions. It was quickly determined that this would not be a quick victory.

In order to take pressure off the units, Billy's regiment was to assault the southern peak of Hill 894. By September 15, the 9th Regiment controlled Hill 894, but for the next two days it had to fight off counterattacks by the North Koreans. And in spite of the success the maneuver failed to relieve pressure on the units still pinned down.

Other units were thrown into the battle. The 1st Battalion, 23rd Regiment, took Hill 931, but was quickly thrown off by a North Korean counterattack. A French battalion charged up a slope to assist the 1st Battalion with fixed bayonets, stabbing North Koreans in their foxholes.

By September 26, the casualties were so high that further assaults were called off. A new plan was devised. Units would move up from the Satae-ri Valley on the east side of Heartbreak Ridge and the 9th Infantry would move up the Muncdung Valley on the west side of Heartbreak Ridge. Air and artillery supported the advances, and the other units continued their fight for the ridge. The operation worked, and the battle was won—but not without cost. The 2nd Division suffered 3,700 casualties, and the estimates for the North Koreans and Chinese were 25,000. It would be Billy's last battle.

Laying Telephone Wire

Fresh from the victory of Heartbreak Ridge, Billy was asked to direct some men as they lay telephone line to an outpost. On the night of October 3, Billy and the three other soldiers began the task. About 50 feet from the outpost they ran out of wire. They radioed back and were told to wait at the position; the wire would be brought to them. Billy laid his rifle on the ground beside him. His buddy dug in next to him.

"All of a sudden bullets were hitting all around me," Billy said. "Then everything quieted down. I knew I was hit, but I couldn't tell where." My buddy said, 'Gaddy, don't leave me. I'm hit.' I told him not to worry; I was hit too."

Billy had been hit in his left leg, and the bullet lodged in his knee. One of the men offered to get help, but Billy knew the Koreans would return soon.

"He picked up my buddy, and I tried to walk," he said. "I just kept falling down. Before long, I was surrounded. I thought that was the end of it."

The Capture

Scared, wounded, and by himself, Gaddy was helpless as the Koreans moved in like lions closing in on their prey.

"They took me down the road, half carrying me and half dragging me," Billy explained. "They took me to a dug-out place, sort of like a cellar, for the night. I was hurting so bad, and it was so cold, somewhere in the thirties. When they came for me the next morning, I figured they would kill me. They stripped me of everything but my field jacket and pants. When one Korean saw that I had a class ring on, they took it too. They even took my boots and socks, and one was fixing to take my field jacket, but I let him know how cold I was, and he let me keep it."

The Interrogation

Billy was transported on a two-wheeled trailer to a Korean military officer, who interrogated him throughout the night. When Billy couldn't tell him what he wanted to know, the officer flashed a pistol in Billy's face.

"He laid the pistol on the table and said, 'I'm going to ask you one more time.' I told him once more that I didn't know anything," Billy said. "That's when he said he would kill me. I cursed him and told him to kill, I thought they were going to anyway. He picked up his gun and said, 'You're a good soldier.' He promised to send me to a POW camp where I would receive food and medical attention."

A Journey Through Hell

The Korean officer called in some men, who placed me on a cow, which would be my mode of transportation to the POW camp, or at least that's what I thought. My leg was bloody and swollen. We traveled all day and most of the night before stopping at a village. I was placed in a village hut and offered boiled rice and weevils to eat. It had been three days since I had eaten, but I still couldn't get the unfamiliar, grotesque food down.

The next morning, I received a fresh cow and started on the journey again. This old Korean man and I went down the road. I hadn't had a drop of water for days. My leg was so swollen it didn't look real. When we came to a river, I remembered I still had on my helmet liner. When we crossed the river, I slid my liner under the water and filled it and turned it up. The old Korean man had been told not to give me water. He saw me and went to muttering something. I knew he would be in trouble, but he couldn't have stopped me.

On the fifth day of my journey I was taken to another village, where I was left on a porch while the Koreans inside the hut discussed what to do with me.

At daylight, I could see smoke. I crawled around into the old hut. My guard was asleep by the mud stove, and another Korean was trying to start the fire. I crawled up to the fire to try to get warm and caught my field jacket on fire. I woke my guard when I was trying to put out the fire. That's when he put me back on the cow to travel again.

In the next village, the hospital was a welcome sight to me, because I knew I was in danger of losing my leg. Except for a few familiar words from my captors now and then, the doctor was the only one I had encountered who could speak English.

He told me he'd have to take my leg off. I was crying, hurting, and suffering. He told me I'd die if he didn't remove it. I told him they were going to kill me anyway. I didn't want to lose my leg.

He talked to some of the other people, then I saw the nurse fixing a needle with medicine in it. The doctor said he had decided to give me shots, and if I wasn't better in the morning, he'd have to do surgery.

Massive doses of penicillin stolen from the American troops were pumped into my leg all night. The treatment was successful, and I was informed by the doctor that I wouldn't lose my leg.

I was allowed to rest during the day, but that night I was transported via truck to another village hospital. Seven days after my capture, starving, barefooted, and freezing, I once again was offered bug-laden rice and water.

All of the rice in Korea was full of bugs. Even though I was starving, I still couldn't eat. One of the nurses saw me. She went and got me a bowl of warm cow's milk and an apple. It was delicious, but a few minutes later, I was hurting so bad inside my stomach, it started coming up.

That night, they brought the rice and water again. They motioned for me to dip the rice in the water. I did what they said, and was able to get it down.

The next move placed me in grave danger. At the hands of a Korean officer, I suffered tremendous abuse and anguish.

They had me sitting by a river creek. Three officers came up, and one of the Koreans walked up and cursed me. He started stomping me and kicking me, then he pointed a pistol right between my eyes. The Chinese officer grabbed his arm and knocked the guy away.

Two Koreans carried me, badly beaten, to the nearby hospital, where I was covered in salve and wrapped in bandages. Nurses rubbed me down with more salve and re-wrapped my bandages daily, using the same bandages over and over. The staple ration of rice, bugs, and water was offered to me. I was suffering from extreme headaches at the time from the inhumane beating.

For ten days, I lay alone on a mud floor, my mind running rampant with thoughts of when the next beating would come and what torturous form it would take. The only relief I had was the remembrances of my mother and of home.

They moved me to a room with four or five wounded Korean soldiers. A Chinese man came in and when he saw me, he grabbed a big knife and was going to cut my throat. One of the Koreans stopped him with a crutch. Shortly afterward, they moved me again.

Every time I was attacked, I was moved to another location. I stayed in about 26 civilian homes while my captors tried to decide what to do with me. A POW camp would have been a relief compared with the constant moving about and physical pain I endured.

Still sore and battered from the recent beating, I was placed in a hospital, where I stayed for one month. I had grown accustomed to the boiled rice, weevils, and water but couldn't eat the raw crawfish I was given.

Homemade crutches helped me hobble around, and in December I was given some padded pants and a heavy shirt to wear. I used my old field jacket to wrap my feet, which were black and blue and swollen from exposure. One tennis shoe, size eight, was given to me for my size nine-and-a-half right foot, but at least it offered warmth to my toes.

In February I got my first bath, which was the most relaxing experience I'd had in Korea. The warm water helped block out the freezing temperatures, but I quickly developed pneumonia. After I was treated, I was moved up to the mountains, where a Korean cut my hair and shaved me with a 50-caliber machine gun clip.

In April I was moved again, and a drunken guard on the truck hit me in the head with a rifle and threatened to shoot me.

Frozen from riding in the snow, I continued to be moved from village to village, aimlessly traveling in circles with no hope of finding a resting place. As I traveled about, Koreans would point their fingers at me, and mock and threaten me.

In June, a little more than eight months after the capture, I was told of an American lieutenant who had been captured. A guard carried me to see him. We talked and talked all day. I went back to the hut, and here came two or three Korean boys, who motioned for me to come because my friend was going to a POW camp. I went back to see the lieutenant. He was crying, and I was too. "Bill, they are sending me to a POW camp." And he told me they were sending me in a week. We said our goodbyes.

In a week's time, they told me I was going to a POW camp. I was tickled to death, but I ended up back in Pyongyang.

Mentally exhausted from promises that never materialized, I then had to endure more physical pain. A doctor tried to remove the bullet from my knee, but to no avail. As soon as the wound was closed, I was sent to dig a supply dump. When the Americans bombed the area, I fought for my life in a mountainside foxhole without any food or water.

When the bombing subsided, I was moved to another village hospital, where the doctor told me the bullet had to come out. Still mentally and physically scarred from the recent surgery attempt, I thought my troubles were worsening, but joy came in the form of a friendly face.

They told me I had a friend to see. It was that same lieutenant. I grabbed him, and he grabbed me. It had been two months since we had said goodbye. They had moved him from place to place just like me, and he never made it to the camp. The lieutenant persuaded the doctor to let him stay with me to help with the operation. The lieutenant and I spent a month and nine days together.

The next morning, shots of Novocaine were used to numb the area surrounding the embedded bullet, but during the surgery the doctor was called away. By the time he returned to resume the operation, the Novocaine had worn off.

The lieutenant tried to keep the flies off of my leg while the doctor was gone. My leg was lying wide open. About 15 minutes later, when the doctor came back, the Novocaine had died. The lieutenant told him to give me some more, but he said he couldn't. I screamed and cried but he dug the bullet out, and it was over.

With no time to recuperate, the lieutenant and I were moved from village to village for about a month digging supply dumps for the Koreans. Then one day we were finally moved to a prison camp.

Camp Three: August 1952

I didn't see the lieutenant again until we were on the ship coming home. They took me to a POW camp and fed me stewed potatoes that morning. I had seen nothing much but boiled rice and weevils the whole time. Those stewed potatoes were awfully good, and I ate my fill. Some of the POWs had turned it down because some of the potatoes were rotten. I thought it was delicious.

I weighed 185 pounds when I was captured, but I was at a mere 103 pounds when I reached the POW camp. My daily rations of fresh vegetables, eggs, and meat satisfied my palate, but my stomach often rejected the rich food.

The POWs were required to be self-sufficient, growing their own food, chopping their own wood, and cooking all of the meals, but this seemed far from torture when compared with my past treatment. During the time in the camp I had malaria fever 14 times.

The End of the War

On July 27, 1953, the peace agreement was signed. The release of prisoners was to take place over the next 60 days. At 11:30 P.M. on August 29, 1953, Billy was released as a prisoner of war. All told he had spent 22 months and 23 days as a POW.

Arrival in the United States

"Just before docking in California, my name was called as one of those who had family waiting on the dock," Billy explained. "I couldn't imagine who

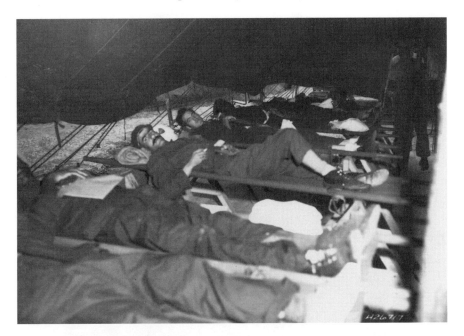

United Nations Forces personnel, captured by the Communists in Korea and repatriated under terms of the POW exchange, Operation Big Switch, lie on stretchers at Panmunjom, awaiting evacuation to hospitals. U.S. Army photo by PFC Joe Adams, August 5, 1953.

in the world was meeting me in California. All of my people were in Tennessee. My sister, her husband, and their little boy were there, and right beside them, the lieutenant, his wife, and his two little girls. I and the lieutenant made a vow to correspond with each other and visit whenever possible, but the lieutenant never answered my letters. I discovered later that the lieutenant died in 1971."

Epilogue

Physical pain and surgery continued for Billy in the States. The nerves in the bottom of his left foot kept him in constant pain, a token of the bullet that had lodged in his knee and the barefooted treks up the mountainsides in below-zero temperatures. The pain from punches, slaps, and kicks to the head and upper body, thought long left in Korea, haunts him today in the form of excruciating headaches. The malnutrition he endured for nearly a year and the bugs and rice that sustained him cause stomach cramps. No matter how much he wants to forget Korea, incessant reminders are all around.

Though still alive, Billy gave his life to his country. The time he served in the Korean War was a nightmare, and the nightmares continue today. The physical pain in his injured leg is secondary to the mental frustration he endures

Billy Gaddy, then and now.

daily. If he watches a war movie, which he often does, he tosses and turns through the night, fighting the ghosts of the past. When he closes his eyes, he can still visualize large rats running across a wire, feeding on drying husks of corn. No matter how full his mind is, he can still hear Korean soldiers shouting obscenities at him, verbally and often physically threatening his life. Though it happened 45 years ago, his safety still is in jeopardy at the hands of a distant enemy.

"When I talk about it, I remember how it felt to think I'd never see tomorrow. I never thought I'd see home again. The Koreans really and truly didn't know what to do with me. Now ... I don't know what to do with myself."

Point of Interest

From December 1950 through January 1951 prisoners in Death Valley were dying at the rate of two to seven a day. On January 21, 1951, 250 of the 300 were either sick or wounded. On March 13, 1951, there were only 109 of them still alive to make the march to Camp Five.

– 8 –

SERGEANT
EUGENE L. INMAN
U.S. ARMY

9th Infantry Regiment, 2nd Infantry Division
Captured at Kuni-ri During an Ambush at the Roadblocks
Prisoner of War
November 30, 1950–August 30, 1953
Death Valley, Camp Four, and Camp Five

A Family of Patriots: 1948

In 1948, shortly after Eugene graduated from high school, he coaxed his mother into signing papers for him to enlist in the U.S. Army. The 18-year-old wanted to follow the family tradition. Four other brothers had served in World War II, and Eugene's mother realized that it was their service that made him anxious to get into the army. She was a little reluctant when she thought back on the war days and of being glued to the radio listening to daily broadcasts about the war. She recalled the time when one son, Roland, was in a bomber that was shot down; she was relieved when she learned that he had survived the crash landing. But nevertheless, Eugene wanted to serve his country, and his mother signed the papers.

Korea: June–November 30, 1950

At the outbreak of the Korean War, Eugene's unit, the 9th Infantry Regiment, was stationed at Fort Lewis, Washington. The unit was supervising and training reservists and conducting the ROTC summer encampment when it was called for overseas duty on July 9, 1950.

This was the first of the divisions to sail for Korea on July 17th–19th. On

August 8, Eugene and the 9th Regiment encountered their first combat near Suga-ri, then, after repulsing enemy counterattacks near Kogana-re, they advanced to Ogong-ni. From this time through August, the Regiment joined the 24th Infantry Regiment and captured Clover Leaf Hill and Maekok village, and repelled counterattacks. As a result of holding back the enemy, they captured more real estate between Ikarikaku and Wokoku. Then they took a defensive position along the Naktong River and once again repelled the enemy. In September, the 9th Infantry took Hill 201, Hyopchon, and Kochang. In October the unit was involved in mop-up operations. Then they moved to Han River for bridge security. In November Eugene's unit moved to the Chongchon River and fought through roadblocks south of Kuni-ri. The unit suffered heavy casualties, and a large number of soldiers was captured. Eugene, after surviving four months of fierce combat, had a new status—prisoner of war.

The Capture: November 30, 1950

The confusion of the ambushes of the roadblocks cut us off from our main lines of departure to our own lines. We were broken up into groups to seek a way out. We ran out of ammunition, and the way out was totally blocked. The order came down, "every man for yourself." Deep down in my heart, I felt that this was it. I prayed, as sincerely as I knew how, and the Lord gave me real peace and calm. About 230 headed up the side of a hill to see if we could get through that way under cover of darkness. I followed them. Then, when we had just about reached the crest, it happened. We were caught in the face of a Communist ambush. Machine gun fire tore at us from all directions. It's hard for me to explain what happened. Even now it seems like a fantastic dream. About all I remember is that I seemed to be looking right into the sights of a Commie machine gun, a gun that was spitting a steady stream of death. Yet nothing hit me. I didn't even get a scratch.

I turned and ran for all I was worth. Looking back, as I tore away, I could see my buddies being bayoneted. So far as I know, I was the only one who escaped death. That was a tremendous moment in my life, and I promised God he could have all of me, always for His glory.

A bit farther on, I ran across a sergeant. Together, we sat down for a short rest. By then, we were completely exhausted.

"You going to surrender?" the Sarge asked me.

"No," I said, and then he got up and started running again. In the moonlight, I saw a Chinese soldier shoot at him and miss. Yet even though I knew I was open to fire myself, I followed him.

"Let's surrender," he begged when I caught up with him.

I still refused. I don't know why I did, really, because it was all up for us. I guess it was just that intense pride every GI has in his heart for America.

Over the brow of a hill, we walked right into a Chinese headquarters encampment. I threw away my M-1 rifle and put up my hands. At that moment I began a way of life no one can really believe possible until he has experienced it himself. I became a prisoner of the Communists.

We were half famished, and the Communists gave us dry bean curd to eat. They marched us to a point of interrogation. We gave them as little information as possible and tried to watch our manners. The Communists were very self-confident in those days, as they were pushing constantly southward, and it looked as though they might drive the United Nations troops right into the ocean.

We were gathered up and placed into a holding area of animal sheds and vacant huts. It was bitter cold, with temperatures well below zero, and we lost all the warm clothing we had to the enemy. I was left with only light clothing. A field jacket was the heaviest article of covering. I also had a fatigue cap and a tattered scarf with no real protection from extreme cold.

After being gathered up we were marched in circles for about 30 days. We always marched at night when the weather was the coldest. My feet, hands, face, and nose were always numb. Night after night I dragged my numb legs beneath me. I prayed to God for strength. Many times I fell asleep as I walked.

With Eugene were some Filipino soldiers who were veterans of the Bataan Death March. They told him that this march was worse.

During the march we truly had no shelter from the elements, and food was provided only at irregular intervals. It consisted of cracked corn, and sometimes the corn was mixed with soy beans. After a couple of days the diet caused me to come down with dysentery, fever, bowl discharge of mucus and blood, abdominal cramps, and rectal pain, and I was always thirsty.

Added to the dysentery and cramps was the brutality by the Chinese soldiers. I had trouble keeping up because of my condition, and the guards would hit me with their rifle butts on the arms, back, head, lower neck region, and shoulders. The pain was almost unbearable.

Even with the horrible conditions, all of us tried to see the bright side of it, and I think a lot of the Chinese got a good dose of American morale as they herded us northward. I met one GI whose heart was really open to the Gospel, and we got to be close friends. He kept talking about how he'd like to get his teeth into some peanut brittle.

"What are you hungry for, Gene?" he asked.

Maybe my mind was playing tricks on me then. I don't know. I said I'd like to get a pound of butter, two bottles of catsup, a box of Aunt Jemima pancake flour, half a pound of link sausage, and four eggs.

"What do you want all that for?" he asked me.

Well, I'd fry the pancakes. Then I'd have a pancake, hamburger, then

Top: Telegram dated January 10, 1951, informing Eugene Inman's mother of his missing in action status. *Bottom:* Telegram dated February 9, 1951, apprising Hazel Inman of her son's status: prisoner of war.

another pancake on top of that, and cover it with the rest. The very thought of it tasted good to me then.

My buddy never got the chance to eat peanut brittle again because he collapsed during the march. We tried to get him up, but his strength was gone. I guess you might say it was merciful when one of the Communist officers killed him. My buddy was among the hundreds who died on the march.

After a month and 500 miles of walking, hunger, cold, and bugs, we reached our first destination—Death Valley.

Death Valley

Death Valley was a deserted mining town in the Pukchin area. We faced the inclement weather, lack of shelter and food. The conditions, along with the fear and beatings by the Chinese, took a large toll on life. Several prisoners a day were dying. For a while, all they fed us was an ear of dented corn each day. We tried to soak it and grind it the best we could to make the stuff palatable. We ate cobs and all. A hungry man isn't too particular.

Sometime later they begin to feed us millet seed. We got 600 calories a day. For a while, especially during the most intensive phase of our brainwashing period, we got up to 1,200 calories. But, for the most part, it was around 600. I began to experience a spastic lower colon because of the poor diet. Medically it is called irritable bowel syndrome. I don't know how I survived Death Valley, but I did.

Even worse than the food was the filth we lived in. It was eight months following my capture before I was permitted to remove my clothes. When I did, they were alive with lice. We slept literally jammed into a tiny room. We worked out a schedule, sleeping first on the left sides, then on our right sides. There wasn't room for anybody to lie flat on his back. Some of the guys got terrible sores from lying in one position on the hard floor.

The first summer was when the bugs really hit us. What I wouldn't have given for a can of DDT to ensure just one good night's sleep. I was there for about three months, and the conditions never changed. I was lucky because they moved me, and had they not I would have died in Death Valley.

Camp Five

I was transferred to another camp at Pyoktong in March 1951. The diet was improved, with corn, millet, and on special occasions a little rice. Still, men died of starvation. Then the camp authorities added bean curd and seaweed to the diet, which helped those who were weak and could not have recovered had it not been for the additions to the diet.

Even with the improvements in the diet, malnutrition was very ghastly in the period from March 1951 to August 1952. I experienced profound changes in the conditions of my body. I could not see well after dark, my sinuses bled, I would urinate blood at various times, and my kidneys hurt. Beriberi began through the severe lack of vitamins, my legs would swell up, and the pain became acute. This "bone aches" pain was not in the swelling but seemed to center in the very bones which no rubbing or any other efforts would relieve.

Peripheral neuropathy, a numbness and pain in my feet, increased and seemed to come as spark interchanges in the nerves. The long trips to carry wood back on my person on ice and snow caused many slips and falls, causing much pain to my extremities.

At the height of the malnutrition I had an extended abdomen, worms in my stool, sores and scales on my body, and my gums and mouth became extremely raw. That was compounded by a Chinese guard who had knocked me around for not being obedient and humble. After the beating when I failed to stand at attention properly, while standing in the snow barefooted, he knocked some of my teeth out. In addition, my ears ached and I suffered hearing loss. My nerves went to pieces.

Indoctrination: August 12, 1952. We spent long hours during the winter months ... we had to sit out in the cold and listen to Red propagandists pitch their hogwash ideas. "We seek the strength and solidarity of the laboring classes of the world," they preached hour after hour. They hated America, of course, and really raved about Paul Robeson, the bad deal the Rosenbergs got, and the Whittaker Chambers fraud, as they called it. For some reason, they seemed to have deep respect for Franklin D. Roosevelt. They despised Eisenhower.

Much of the time I spent as a prisoner of the Communists is all blank to me. I must have gone for weeks in a total mental vacuum. The Communists did all they could to make it difficult for us to in any way acclimate ourselves to our incarceration. There is a Chinese opera called "The White Haired Girl." To an Occidental, it's a mess of discord—harmony in reverse, you might say. They about drove us crazy, playing that thing over and over.

Little by little, however, I did get hold of myself. I never could take for granted the atrocities inflicted upon many of my buddies, but I did realize I might be in the hands of the Reds for a long time and might as well make the best of it. Besides, I had the Lord with me. Time and again, it was His strength alone that saw me through. For I had my Bible with me—the Bible that I now treasure above everything else I own.

I went against the camp authorities and the Communist indoctrination. I held my Christian faith. I was soon recognized as a reactionary.

While the Reds concentrated on the political brainwashing of his fellow prisoners, they paid special attention to efforts to destroy the sergeant's ideas of God.

They waved pistols in my face and threatened to kill me. They said to show them my God. If He really exists, point him out.

The Reds always had a reason for everything they did, even when they killed many of my buddies. They wanted to get my Bible away from me and made all kinds of accusations. One officer held a cocked pistol at my head and demanded that I give it up, cleverly inferring that to do so meant I also forfeited my Christian faith. I still wonder sometimes why he didn't fire the gun, because I didn't give him my Bible. My reactionary status landed me in solitary confinement for 90 days. Those 90 days, after all that I had endured, were a worse hell. I had nightmares, flashbacks, and insomnia. The stress caused me to be jumpy, and this was aggravated by cold sweats. This was my payment for being incorrigible and rebellious.

Camp Four

Those of us who actively resisted the Communist program were sent to a new camp. We were taken by boat up the Yalu River for several miles and then walked to a place called Wiwon. This camp was to break our morale and spirit by making as many people as possible suspicious of each other and to break down any kind of leadership position.

Just as I arrived at the new camp Joseph Stalin died. It was unbelievable the way it hit those Chinese and North Korean soldiers. He had a tremendous hold on his followers.

The one good thing that happened was that the diet was improved because the peace talks were positive and the tide of battle began to turn. But as the rate of death decreased, our physical conditions were still poor. Then Operation Little Switch came along, and the Chinese even gave us some spending money. Our food rations improved even more.

Deep in my heart, I began to become impatient for freedom. God had really spoken to my heart during those years, and I dedicated it anew to Him. Once safely back in America, I wanted to begin immediately preparing myself to preach his unsearchable riches.

I decided to try to hold worship services for the prisoners there in camp. I had to get permission from the officials. We were in a camp directed by Chinese Communists, and I prayed hard that they would give me permission to start holding these meetings. They were very skeptical, but in answer to my earnest prayer, they gave their reluctant consent.

The guys were a little hesitant about it at first, but soon we had a full-fledged congregation. Some of the men donated cigarette papers—it was the only paper we had—and we printed hymns on them. "The Old Rugged Cross" was a favorite of everybody.

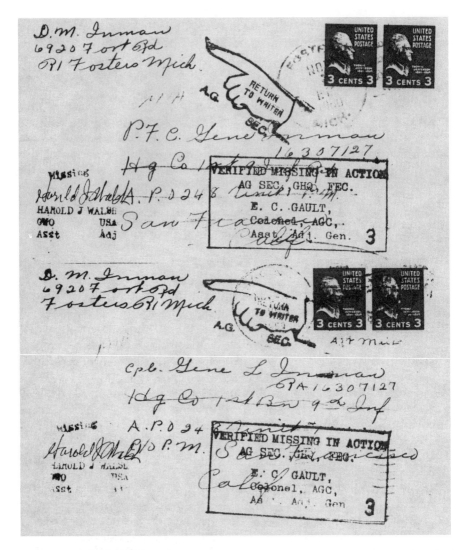

Returned envelopes, dated 1950, bearing stamps that verify Eugene Inman is missing in action.

After we sang a few hymns, we would pause for silent prayer. Catholics and Protestants both bowed to pray. Then I would give the message. My first text was John 14:1. Tears came to the eyes of those men, as, with my faltering tongue, I told them what Christ had done for them. I expect to meet many of those men in heaven because God's word will not return unto Him void.

Almost as thrilling as these meetings were the chances I had to occasionally witness to the Communist themselves. There was a Chinese named Scarface. He had a bad scar that he picked up fighting against the Japanese in World War II. He became so friendly to us that he saw to it we got secret food supplements. One officer became so interested in the salvation of his soul that they had to ship him off to another camp. Maybe they had him executed. I hope not. But if they did, I like to believe that he really opened his heart to the Savior and is in heaven.

After the Panmunjom talks got under way, the Reds were a bit easier on us. They let us have recreation periods, mainly so they could take propaganda pictures. I had played on a Detroit Free Press baseball team that went to the small-fry championship finals, so it really felt good to get outside for some fun, even though I had lost 135 pounds and was suffering from internal bleeding.

Freedom at Last: August 30, 1953

After being a prisoner of war for 34 months Eugene got the news that the war was over. Like many of the other POWs he was thrilled, but it was still hard to believe that this living hell was soon to be over. The prisoners were given some new clothing and a better diet, and then on August 30, 1953, Eugene and the other prisoners were exchanged at Panmunjom. They crossed the Freedom Bridge and were placed in American hands. Eugene cried like a baby.

The ordeal wasn't over, however. Being a prisoner of war under the Chinese Communists had taken its toll on Eugene. "This should have been a great time for me," Eugene explained, "but I felt a deep sense of anxiety and distrust. I felt very hostile at some of the things that I was involved in. I expected a very thorough physical exam and care for my aches and pains. Instead, I was pushed through the exam, placed on a helicopter, and sent aboard a slow ship to the States. Slow, because they spent most of their time picking our brains. When we landed in San Francisco, I was given partial pay and sent on my way."

Eugene's family support and love and his trust in God helped him to adjust to his new life of freedom. While Eugene was on work details in prison camp he dreamed of a "nice girl." When he got home he asked a friend to find one. The friend introduced him to her cousin,

Eugene Inman

Rosemary Miller. The couple met in church, and the next day Eugene proposed to her. They were married on November 28, 1953.

There was another issue that the ex–POW had to deal with. All the time after Eugene's release he was having a struggle with his conscience. Before his army days, he had, he says, "never been sincerely religious." But now, in his own words, he felt he "had experienced the touch of God." He felt the call to the pulpit. The following poem by Frances Augermayer, published in a World War II era *Stars and Stripes*, still expresses his feelings about his faith. Eugene says many soldiers carried this poem with them into battle.

… And God Was There

Look, God, I have spoken to you,
But now, I want to say, "How do you do?"
You see, God they told me you didn't exist,
And, like a fool, I believed all this.

Last night from a shell hole I saw your sky–
I figured right then they had told me a lie,
Had I taken time to see things You made,
I'd have known they weren't calling a spade a spade.

I wonder, God, if You'd shake my hand;
Somehow, I feel that You'll understand.
Funny, I had to come to this hellish place
Before I had time to see your face.

Well, I guess there isn't much more to say,
But I'm sure glad, God, I met You today.
I guess the "zero hour" will soon be here,
But, I'm not afraid since I know You're near.

The signal: Well, God, I'll have to go;
I like You lots, this I want you to know.
Look now, this will be a horrible fight—
Who knows, I may come to Your house tonight.

Though I wasn't friendly to You before,
I wonder, God, if You'd wait at Your door.
Look, I'm crying. Me! Shedding tears—
I wish I had known You these many years.

Well, I have to go now, God. Good-bye!
Strange, since I met You, I'm not afraid to die.

Ministry at Olivet: September 1954

Eugene entered the Olivet Nazarene College in Kankakee, Illinois to become a minister. After graduation at Olivet, Eugene served three more years

```
    .DEA015 SPF135 RA025                    1953 AUG 30  AM  8  26
P.WA096 XV GOVT PD=WUX WASHINGTON DC 30    651AME=
MRS HAZEL P INMAN=DELIVER IMMEDIATELY=
     6920 FORT RD FOSTERS MICH=
THE SECRETARY OF THE ARMY HAS ASKED ME TO INFORM YOU THAT
YOUR SON SGT INMAN EUGENE L WAS RETURNED TO MILITARY
CONTROL IN KOREA AND WILL BE RETURNED TO THE UNITED STATES
BY SURFACE TRANSPORTATION AT AN EARLY DATE. YOU WILL BE
ADVISED OF ARRIVAL DATE=
        WM E BERGIN MAJOR GENERAL USA THE ADJUTANT
        GENERAL OF THE ARMY=                   72139

        THE COMPANY WILL APPRECIATE SUGGESTIONS FROM ITS PATRONS CONCERNING ITS SERVICE
```

Telegram dated August 30, 1953, announcing Eugene Inman's imminent return.

at the Church of the Nazarene Seminary and then became a minister, dedicating his life to God.

Epilogue

Time has passed since those days of war, and much has changed in the world. But for Eugene much has not changed. Eugene still has flashbacks of his time in hell as a POW; he still suffers from some medical problems associated with his time as a POW. He is still married to Rosemary, and his faith in God is just as strong today as it was that day in 1950 when he was the only one to escape death, when he promised God He could have all of him, always for His glory.

Points of Interest

Those prisoners who stayed in the mining camps suffered the following diseases: 100 percent had dysentery at one time or another, 100 percent suffered cold injury, of which 15 percent had tissue loss, 25–30 prisoners developed infectious hepatitis, of which 50 percent died, and 100–150 prisoners contracted pneumonia, from which only six survived.

Marijuana was a definite problem in camps One, Three and Five; 5–30 percent of the prisoners used it regularly. The Chinese in charge of the camps made unsuccessful attempts to stop the use of the drug.

– 9 –

PRIVATE
PAUL H. SMITH
U.S. ARMY

19th Regiment, 24th Division
Captured During a Battle at Pusan
Prisoner of War
July 30, 1950–
Camp Four and Camp Five

Twice a POW: January 2, 1943, October 1944

Paul has had many experiences in his lifetime with the military, war, and prison camps, because he was a POW twice in two different wars. Although this story will deal with his experiences as a POW in Korea, we must start at the beginning of his military career, in 1943, during World War II. At the age of 22 Paul was drafted on January 2, 1943. He failed the physical exam because of his teeth and was sent home. The next day he went to the U.S. Army recruiting office and was enlisted.

In May 1944, after his training, he was shipped to the European theater. He trained with the 76th Division but fought with the 79th Division. Paul was captured near the Rhine River when his patrol was ambushed by German soldiers. When his parents were notified, they were told that he was dead.

Paul marched for days without food until he and the other prisoners arrived at Stalag XIIA. The conditions were bad and the food was scarce. The Germans needed food for their troops, and manpower was short, so they used prisoners to take care of the farming. Paul had received a battlefield commission and didn't have to work because of his officer status. However, Paul volunteered because he figured he would be able to get more to eat.

Paul began to make an escape plan. He watched for several days while working in the fields. There was a forest a couple of hundred yards from his location. One evening, just before dusk, Paul got his chance and darted across the field into the woods.

Paul walked at night and hid in barns during the day. He grabbed what food he could from gardens along the way. After a few days he thought he was in France and stopped at a house and asked for some milk. While he drank his milk, the resident called for the Nazi soldiers. He was still in Germany.

Paul was placed in solitary confinement for 13 days without food or water. He was beaten during that time on a couple of occasions. Finally, he was released from confinement. The other prisoners took Paul into the barracks and took care of him until he got some of his strength back.

It was a couple of months before the Nazis would let Paul work outside the camp again. As soon as they did, he started planning for another escape. It wasn't long before he had escaped again. This time he decided he wouldn't talk to anyone. He had a plan: he would act as if he were crazy. When he came across anyone who wanted to talk to him, he would just wave and keep going. He stole a motorcycle and rode it until he ran out of gas. Then one day he was walking along a road and heard a car coming. Before he could get away, people in the car spotted him. When they asked him who he was, he couldn't talk— he was so scared he just mumbled. They took him back to their car, and he found out that it was a French command car. He had made it to freedom.

Korea: The Second War, Pusan Perimeter, 1950

On January 10, 1946, Paul was discharged from the service. He returned home and worked at different jobs over the next four years. Then the Korean War broke out. Paul enlisted once again. After training, Paul was assigned to the 24th Division and shipped to Korea. His unit was sent immediately to the front, which was located at the southern tip of South Korea—Pusan.

The North Koreans were advancing rapidly toward the south, pushing the U.S. Army toward the sea. Although a number of defensive maneuvers slowed the advance some they did little to help the Americans hold any ground. Pusan was the last chance for the Americans to maintain a foothold on any real estate in South Korea. A perimeter was set up along the Naktong River, and orders were that there would be no further withdrawals. "We were able to stop them," Paul remembered, "but not without intense fighting. The North Koreans would take a little ground at night and we would take it back during the day. They would send wave after wave of North Korean soldiers, and most of the time we would just run out of ammo and then be overrun.

Night after night when the light was gone we would come under attack. They came at us blowing bugles and shouting. They fired red and green flares and continued mounting attack after attack." And then the unit was overrun. This time Paul had another "second" in his life. Not only was he fighting in his second war, but he was about to become a prisoner of war for the second time in his life.

The Capture

It was July 30, 1950 when Paul was captured. The North Koreans came in wave after wave, and Paul's unit ran low on ammunition. Then Paul was wounded in the head. He was unconscious for a while, and when he woke up the North Koreans were everywhere. He had been in Korea for three months and he was a prisoner of war for the second time in his life. "I was in a daze from the wound. Everything around me was like a fog," Paul explained. "The North Koreans made me stand up so they could tie my hands behind my back. I fell, and a North Korean soldier started hitting me in the back with his rifle butt. I was real weak, but I managed to get back to my feet. They tied my hands with communications wire and started marching me down the hill. I thought I was the only one they got until I got to the bottom. Then I saw several more of the men had been captured.

The March

They started marching us. We walked all night. I don't know how I managed. At times I would not know from one point to another how I got there.

During the day we would hole up in Korean huts. The North Koreans were hiding from the American planes. During the day we slept, at night we marched. We were given very little food or water during the march. To this day I don't know where I got my strength, but many couldn't hold up. When one of the men would fall out, the North Koreans would just shoot him and leave him lay. Within a few days we all had dysentery, body lice, and infection from our wounds. We got no medical attention at all. The one thing we did get was a rifle butt in the head or back if we weren't marching fast enough. I never thought I would feel good about arriving at another prison camp, but when we arrived at the prison camp, it was a pleasant sight, but only because we knew we wouldn't have to march again.

Camp Four

Paul and the other survivors of the march arrived at Camp Four, Pyoktong, North Korea, after about three weeks of marching. Camp Four was located on the banks of Wiwon Gang River. The camps were surrounded by six- to eight-foot barbed-wire fences. There were guards posted at several locations around the camp. "We were in bad shape," Paul said. "We were starved and suffering from infection, dysentery, and pneumonia. They fed us rice twice a day. We got some water to clean our wounds and some medicine to fight the infection, but it didn't help much. We got to rest for a while, and then they began to make us work in the fields. A number of the prisoners died while we were there. They died from starvation and disease. I was getting my strength back and then one day they came in and got me. I was being moved."

Camp Five

Paul was moved to Camp Five, which was also located in Pyoktong. The camp was separated from the town by a four- or five-foot barbed-wire fence. A guard staff of about 200 men was provided for approximately 12 guard posts at the camp. "We were fed rice at this camp also," Paul said,

Men were dying fast in the camp. They were dying from starvation, dysentery, and pneumonia. I had dysentery, but I walked around and kept moving. It helped some. Then a couple of months after I was in the camp they started to give us hard corn and some beans. I was getting a little strength back. There were five of us who had been trying to find a way to escape. We figured if we were going to be successful we'd better do it soon. We had a little of our strength back, but no one could predict what would happen in the future in this prison camp.

Aerial photo of POW Camp #5.

The Escape

One morning the Koreans moved a group of us to a nearby farm. We were supposed to work the fields. I guess the Koreans thought we were too weak and scared to try and escape, but that was their mistake. There were five of us watching some trucks that had been parked on a road near the field. I don't know to this day why they were there, but the Korean guards seemed to be occupied with themselves. We worked our way as close to the trucks as we could, and then we made a run for it. The guards spotted us, but not before we got a good jump on them. They opened fire and started chasing us. They hit one of the men, and we picked him up and kept on running. We jumped in this truck and took off down the road. We drove south as fast as the truck would run and got away from the guards. We never stopped for anything until we ran out of gas. We left the bullet-riddled truck in a ditch along the road. We kept on moving as fast as we could, carrying the wounded guy with us. We were in too big of a hurry to notice at the time, but the wounded prisoner was dead. He had been shot right through the chest and probably died instantly but we hadn't noticed. We walked for most of the night, and the next morning we started down a hill and I saw the most beautiful sight in my life, American troops. We had made it to freedom.

Return Home

For the next few months Paul spent most of his time in hospitals in Japan and Hawaii recuperating. He had lost 60 pounds, and suffered from amoebic dysentery, beriberi, and pneumonia. The doctors said he was lucky to be alive. Paul's family was notified that he had been found. It wasn't until he was in contact with them that he discovered that his mother had been told he was missing in action and presumed dead. It was the second time she had been given the tragic news, only to find out later that Paul was alive.

After a few months of recuperation Paul was sent home. He was reunited with his family and was discharged from the U.S. Army. Paul had twice been a POW, his family had been notified that he was dead twice, and he had escaped twice. Paul's comment about it: "I just wasn't a very fast runner."

Epilogue: 1961

In 1961 Paul's mother was contacted by the Illinois Veterans Commission. The commission wanted Mrs. Smith to know that the State of Illinois was engaged in the administration of benefits to Korean veterans. They told her that the veterans were eligible or the veterans' beneficiaries were eligible. Since she was a beneficiary, she would be eligible. The commission still had Paul listed as having been killed in action.

Paul Smith, far right, is pictured with other members of the O'Fallon of the Okow Chapter of the American Ex-Prisoners of War, Inc. The other members (*from left*) **are Vince Rolves, Cebert Turner, Willie Sparlin and Benjamin Pedigo.**

Points of Interest

No group of men in the history of the U.S. Army has been studied as closely as those men who served in Korea. An investigation was conducted in 1954: 425 ex–POWs—215 still on active duty and 210 already discharged—were judged worthy of further study as possible collaborationists. Of the 215 cases of suspects on active duty, 82 were approved for court-martial. Of those, 47 cases were approved by the Army Board of Collaboration for court-martial. Fourteen actually went to trial, resulting in 11 convictions and three acquittals. Eight of those were enlisted men, while the other three were officers.

In a Korean prison camp, simply to survive every day was heroism, and a victory might have been in quietly encouraging a buddy to go on living when his toes were frozen or his dysentery had enervated him. To resist, and even antagonize the captor, as many did, is nothing short of heroic. Instead of perceiving this, the press often dwelt on the sensational, such as lack of escapes, the germ warfare, the confessions of a few, the mysterious brainwashing, or the brutality of the captors.

– 10 –

SERGEANT
DONALD L. SLAGLE
U.S. ARMY

19th Infantry Regiment, 24th Division
Captured During a Battle with Chinese Soldiers
Prisoner of War
November 5, 1950–August 1953
Camp Five

High School Graduation and a Trip
to See a Brother: May–July 1948

In May 1948 Donald graduated from Narka High School in Kansas. His parents didn't have the money for him to go to college or to a trade school. Donald went to work part-time at his father's garage pumping gas. In early July Donald got restless, as he explained, "I told Mom I wanted to go to Salina to see brother Milt, who was in the Air Force there. So, Mom gave me money for the bus fare. At this time, I talked to Milt and decided to join the service."

Basic Training: Fort Knox, Kentucky, July 1948

"Before I knew it, I was on my way to Fort Knox, Kentucky, for seven weeks of basic training," Donald said. "Then I got nine days' furlough. The night before I left Fort Knox, the guy sleeping in the bunk above me went AWOL and took my billfold with my $75 in it, which was my month's pay. So I wired home for money for bus fare. I only got to spend two days at home, as it took the other seven days for travel. At this time, we said our goodbyes, and I told Mom not to worry, that I'd be back. Brother Vern took me to Belleville to the train. From Belleville, I went to Colorado until December 1949. Then I received orders for Fort Lawton, Washington, for overseas duty in Japan."

The 21-Day Voyage: December 1949

Donald boarded the USS *Freeman* and befriended George Schoonover from Sardis, Ohio. The two became best friends and stuck together during the voyage. A few days out to sea they got their first taste of seasickness. "The mess hall was in the middle of the ship," Don explained.

> Everything like tables and chairs were fastened down. George and I had just gotten our trays and food when this guy upchucked all his food. We just got up and ran up on deck. That's when I almost got sick. We never went down to eat again. We had our own potato chips and candy bars. Later we got into a typhoon. There was a lot of wind, and the ship just rocked back and forth. People really got sick—what a mess! We slept in hammocks, and I thank God I had the top one. They gave us seasickness pills, which were nothing more than aspirins, but a lot of the troops believed they really helped them. We threw ours overboard; I never did like to take them.

Japan: The 19th Infantry Regiment, 24th Division, January 1949–June 1950

On the twenty-first day the USS *Freeman* pulled into dock at Yokohama, Japan. Don had his first taste of Japanese culture and his first tour of Japan. "My brother Vern had been there before, so he told me about the Japs' habits, like picking up cigarette butts and never using a bathroom," Don said.

> They just squat and do their job, and go on. The women seemed to be the worst. I don't know who picks up the mess. Off the ship, we were loaded on a truck that took us to a train station. On the train trip, we went through Hiroshima where they dropped the atom bomb. There was nothing there, just a sign with the name on it. We went underground through a tunnel for five miles that took us to the island of Kyushi and the town of Beppu. It wasn't much of a town. We finally got to the 19th Regiment, 24th Division. George and I got to be in the same barracks; we also got chosen as squad leaders. He had the second and I had the third, which consisted of about 15 or 16 men to each squad. Master Sergeant Point was our platoon leader. He was a good sergeant. He was a veteran of World War II and had been in the service for 18 years. He sure knew a lot about hand-to-hand combat, but no wonder. He had a bayonet scar on his left cheek from a fight in World War II. Our commanding officer was Lieutenant McGill—wasn't very big but sure was nice.
>
> George and I stayed on the base most of the time. It was about six months before we ever went downtown because of the diseases the Jap women had—venereal, syphilis, etc. Some of the troops ended up with it. After they

were treated in front of everyone, it made you think you'd better leave your pants on!

Life on base wasn't bad. I always wore army clothes from head to toe. I always had on army shorts; the rest of the men had on white ones. I made Colonel Orders four times, which consisted of reporting to the colonel who was in charge of the 19th Regiment. I had to drive the jeep for him. He must have been afraid of my driving 'cause he told me to go back to the barracks and take the day off. I was lucky, though, 'cause I spent six years in the service and never had to pull KP or guard duty. The Japs came in everyone's compounds, polishing up the area. Later, two for each barracks came in and ironed our clothes, and polished our boots for 300 yen. For one dollar of our money, you got 350 yen in their money. At the PX, one carton of cigarettes cost $1.50. Some guys took them to town and sold them for 1,800 yen, but you'd better not get caught selling them or any other army supplies.

George and I were in Company C. They had a plaque saying "Best Unit of the Month." Our C Company had it most of the time. Finally, George and I had enough courage to go downtown. Outside the gate, Japs had a rickshaw to take you and it only cost 350 yen, so we took it downtown. The cars were all charcoal burners with lots of smoke. The streets were all dirt. They had fruit and food stands all over the place. We never ate anything. As we walked down the street, we had to be careful because if you weren't careful you would step in a pile of shit. They used oxen to pull a wagon with a barrel on it. They called it a honey cart, which was filled with human fertilizer to use on their rice paddies. What a smell! They caught fish and didn't clean them—put them on their roofs to dry and then would eat them. We saw the sights, but we also learned something. If you sat down and drank saki, you wouldn't stand on your feet for a while.

The Korean War: The Front Lines, July 1950

After the Korean War broke out on June 25, 1950, the 24th Infantry was deployed from Japan and arrived at Pusan on July 13. The unit was formed into Task Force Able on July 18 and had the responsibility of setting a defense line to protect the 25th Division's left flank in the Sanhji and Hamchang region. Don and his friend George had just returned from three weeks of NCO school in Kokura, Japan, when they got the news about Korea. "Just got back from NCO school, and they said we were going to Korea because the North had attacked the South," Don recalled.

The next morning we were loaded on trucks and went to Oita, Japan, where we boarded a landing craft with tanks, trucks, etc., and sailed for Pusan, Korea. We landed the next day and started walking for about five miles and were then loaded on a train. Didn't go far, though, we stopped and

Donald Slagle, right, and Glen House stand at attention in Beppu, Japan, before departing for Korea.

heard a shot. This South Korean had shot the engineer because he was a North Korean. I couldn't tell the difference between them, but they could. So we had to get off the train and walk to the Kum River, which was the front lines in South Korea territory. The roads were like ox trails, just a path. There were some big hills by the Kum River, and that's where we dug in. After dark, the company sent out scouts. I was one of them. We crossed the river, and about a mile north we could hear them talking. We just made contact and went back to report it. Early the next morning, everything broke out. There were too many Koreans and not enough of us. It was reported that they had two divisions to our little regiment. Lieutenant McGill gave us an order to be passed down—everyone for yourself. Some got out, a lot got killed. I got wounded as I crawled over a dead body. I and four buddies stayed put until dark. At dark, we started to move to a hillside. About ten minutes later, planes came in and started to destroy the vehicles, jeeps, etc. I had a compass, so we started south. After about three miles, my pants were rubbing my wounds, so I had my pant legs removed. We were behind enemy lines for days, just traveling at night. One morning we could see the airport. We made it just in time; they were moving out. They put me in a jeep and gave me a shot, and that's all I remember. I woke up on a British Red Cross ship headed for Japan. I went to the 35th Station Hospital in Tokyo on August 10, 1950. I was only there for two weeks, and I was sent back to my outfit in Korea. I couldn't walk too good yet, and the new commanding officer, Captain Louis Rockwert, wasn't going to send me back, but I told him I could make it.

I wanted to get back to my buddies. George was still there. He got out at the Kum River; I should have stayed with him. We talked for a long time. He was in a battle while I was in the hospital. Master Sergeant Point was all right too. Lieutenant McGill, guys named Oles, Peterson, Caloway, and probably about 20 others were missing.

The Last Battle: November 1950

Later we had the North Koreans on the run. Orders came to withdraw, so we did and that's when the Chinese entered the war. This was when I wrote my last letter home. I told Mom everything was quiet and I was okay. Later that day, there was troop movement in front of us—probably about 700 yards. Sergeant Point said the captain thought they were South Koreans on a withdrawal, but it turned out they were Chinese. They got behind us, so we started shooting. Sergeant Point had a radio and found out that companies A, B, and D, heavy weapons companies, had all withdrawn, so it was just our Company C fighting for our lives. Sergeant Point got information over the radio that companies A and B were going to counterattack, but they never did.

The Capture: November 5, 1950

My buddy George said, "Slagle, let's go!" He went on. Sergeant Point got hit, and it was too late for me to go now. I checked the sergeant, and he was dead. I crawled about 50 yards when I saw a trench, so that's where I went. They had us surrounded, so one of the guys put a white handkerchief on his rifle for surrender. I had a scope on my M-1 rifle, so I took my bayonet and hid it, took the trigger apart and threw it away. Someone dropped a .45 pistol, so I picked it up. They shouted for us to put our hands on our heads. I still had the .45 in my hand over my head. One of the Chinese grabbed it and pointed it at me. I thought I was a goner. They took us to the road, took our watches, billfolds, and everything else we had. Then they tied our hands behind our backs. They even took our helmets.

Some planes were coming over our heads, so they put us in a wooded area until the planes left. Later, we went out on the road again. There were 18 of us. We had to make a stretcher for Lieutenant Funchess, who had a leg wound. Then we started walking, taking turns carrying him.

The day was November 5, 1950. I kept track of the days because November 15 was my birthday. On my birthday we were still walking—mostly going around in circles. We were all losing weight because we had nothing to eat.

We used snow to kill our thirst. If you fell behind, you were dead. They shot the ones who couldn't keep up. We were going through a village, and civilians were throwing rocks at us. English-speaking Chinese said we had about two more miles to go.

Prison Camp Five

We got to the village of Pyoktong. Our POW camp was Number Five— next to the Yalu river. Right across the river were the Manchurian Mountains of China. The huts we were in had dirt floors made of straw and mud and limbs from the trees. They had straw roofs. The room was ten by ten feet with 17 of us in each hut. We had no heat and had to sit up to sleep. The temperature was 30–40 below zero, and everyone was wearing summer clothing. The first meal consisted of soupy rice. It was the same twice a day.

The town of Pyoktong was located at the base of the peninsula on the Yalu River, and the town was occupied by a large number of Chinese troops, which added security to the camp. High fences were installed around the camp. All the guards and the commander of the camp lived on the hill in our camp. The guards' huts were about 50 yards apart.

There were separate compounds for the POW officers: U.S. Negro Compound EM, U.S. Caucasian Turkish Compound EM, U.S. Caucasian Compound EM, UN Sergeants' Compound, UN Officers' Compound.

Death of a Friend. The Chinese brought more POWs to our camp. This was the latter part of December 1950. I heard my name called. It was my buddy, George. I was really glad to see him alive. He said his ulcer was really bothering him. We talked for a while, and the Chinese took his group to a different compound. At this time, his rank was master sergeant. I never got to see him again. I was told that he died in the middle of January. The rice wasn't good for his ulcers. I cried for days over his death and the fact that I never got to see him again. He was buried across the Yalu River on a hillside. The ground was frozen so hard that the graves were only about two feet wide, six feet long, and one foot deep. They just covered them up with rocks and snow. The guards wouldn't let us dig any longer. They said it was a waste of time.

Indoctrination. The Chinese Communists immediately began an indoctrination program when we arrived at the camp. We had indoctrination seven days a week. We started with lectures about Communism versus capitalism. We would have lectures, then go back with one of the Chinese and discuss what we had learned. It didn't work for the most part! They tried to turn the whites against the Negroes, and when that failed they tried to turn the Negroes against the whites. That didn't work for the most part either! The indoctrination lasted for two years, and the only thing that was good about it was it helped pass the time.

We did have a few informers. We called them turncoats. They were in a lot better shape than we were because they ate better. They ate with the Chinese. They were aiding the Communist propaganda activities in writing information, signing peace petitions, and in broadcasting. Some of the white people were worse than the blacks. They thought they were so smart and knew they wouldn't be touched, since they worked for the Chinese. They also mistreated some of the POWs at times.

Some of the informers' names in our compound were Bachelor, Moore, Douglas, and Skinner. These were the ones most of us knew. They never came back to the U.S.A.—they went to China, except for Moore.

Camp Five Has a New Name: Death Camp. We nicknamed the commander of our company the Screaming Skull. That's what he did every morning at roll call. During the cold weather, from November 1950 to March 1953, about 1,600 GIs died, most from starvation. As a result, we named Number Five the Death Camp. The ones who couldn't eat their rice died, some got pneumonia, dysentery, and tapeworms. The lice would lay their eggs in the seams of our clothing. When they hatched they would crawl on us and suck the blood from our bodies. The only way we had to delouse was to pick the lice from our clothing. We never got them all. There was no sanitation. We never got to wash our hands, face, or hair until the spring of 1952. They told us we could bathe in the river. I jumped in, clothes and all.

One of the guys drowned in the river while we were taking a bath. They tried to get him out, but he was wedged between two large rocks. The next day he was floating near the bank. They put him on a small boat and buried him on Boot Hill.

Some of us got night blindness real bad. Another problem was tapeworms. I traded my boots to a Turk for two balls of garlic and ate it all. That's what got rid of my worms and helped save my life. I pulled out some of the worms with my hands. Some were six to eight inches long and one quarter inch in diameter. It was the best thing I did because once you got sick, there wasn't any medical treatment of any kind. You just weren't going to make it, and all the POWs knew this. They were burying GIs every day. At least ten and sometimes more.

A Letter from Home. At night I prayed I would make it home someday. I thought of all the people in Narka and Hubbell that I knew, trying to see how many names I could remember. A Chinese leader held mail call, and he told us when it was time to write letters. The materials were passed out to us—straight pens and ink. The materials were later collected for the next time. Our mail was all opened by the Chinese and later given to us whenever they wished. A letter from home in 1952 sure did help me. My mom wrote a lot of letters because my brother Delbert mailed them for her, but I only got a few of them. I tried to read the ones I got over and over. I also got a Dear John letter from my girlfriend in school. Sure glad I wasn't married. A lot of guys got Dear John letters from their wives.

Mail Call: A Needle and Thread. A buddy of mine received a needle and thread in the mail. He had part of a blanket, so we made some socks. He had also had a multipurpose knife with scissors in it. We put our feet on the blanket and cut about two inches bigger around our feet—made the back part and top and sewed them together. Maybe they didn't look the best, but at least they were warm. In our camp we couldn't have any fires. Wintertime temperatures were 20 and 30 degrees below zero. Body heat was how we survived. However, we wanted to start a fire. That was a mistake because we got caught stealing firewood for a fire. The guards made us stand out in the snow, barefooted, for three hours. Those homemade socks really came in handy after that.

Work Details: The Turnip Hole. The Chinese picked about eight POWs to unload barges in the spring and summer months. They had supplies for the front lines and food for themselves—like chickens, potatoes, rice, etc. If you took something and got caught, you got put in the turnip hole. It was about 20 feet deep and three feet in diameter. The good Lord was looking out for us because those of us on the detail never got caught. It was later that I got caught trying to steal potatoes. They put me in the hole. It was like being buried alive. I don't know how I stood it.

Marijuana. Some of the guys smoked marijuana. It grew wild everywhere over there, and the Turks knew all about it. They would mix it with leaf tobacco the Chinese gave them. They used a Chinese newspaper to roll their cigarettes in. There would be about ten of them passing it around to everyone. The Chinese didn't care. They would just laugh at them.

A POW named Andy Anderson really got hooked on smoking the marijuana. He was where he wouldn't eat—just skin and bones—and was losing his eyesight. You could tell he was smoking it because his eyes were always glassy. At the first POW reunion I saw his wife. Andy had already passed away.

Dogfights and Bombing Runs. We watched a lot of dogfights during the day when the jets were flying over our area. The Chinese pilots flew low over us, going south, and in about an hour they came back, with American planes chasing them. We saw some shot down. Two of the Chinese planes hit a mountain. One of the pilots bailed out, and some of the Chinese in our camp got in a boat and went over there. We didn't know what happened to the pilot.

During the night, you could hear the bombers above. They were just roaring and humming, unloading bombs over the mountains. They must have hit ammunition dumps because the sky was just on fire. This went on for months.

Good News: Stalin is Dead, The War Is Over, 1953. We were called into formation one day, and the Screaming Skull told us that Stalin had died. Immediately, without any thought, we all raised our arms and cheered. He went into a rage and we were put on details moving large rocks from one place to another. It didn't last too long, though, because the war was coming to a close.

The day before the Chinese told us the war was over, we knew it anyway. Our jets flew over our camp at about 30 feet high. They were turning and flapping their wings trying to give us the signal. They made two passes that way. The next day the Chinese told us the war had ended.

Repatriation: August 1953

The peace treaty was signed on July 27, 1953. They took the wounded ones out first. Later in August, we walked for miles, but no one minded because we knew we were about to be free. Later, we ended up being put on trucks and were taken to Freedom Village. They had a sign set up kind of like an arch that said "Repatriation Here," with two North Koreans on the north side and two GIs on the south side. They also had a bunch of tents set up. When we got into American hands, everyone was so happy. It was great to see the American flag. They took the seriously ill and moved them to hospitals in Japan. The rest of us got our hair and beards cut—first time in three years. The hair that they cut off of us was just loaded with lice, and the hair on the ground was moving around from the lice. We were sprayed and given new clothes. From Panmunjom, all of us were moved to the embarkation port of Inchon by helicopter. We boarded the ship USS *General Hase* for the States.

The Golden Gate: The Trip Back to Kansas

I don't remember how many days it took us on the water coming back, but no one really cared. We knew we were going home. Coming into California, we went by Alcatraz prison. I remember comments that some GIs, including myself, would rather be there than Korea. We went under the Golden Gate and docked in San Francisco. They called our names, and we departed the ship. My folks were there, my brother Ernie and his wife, and my cousin Don Young. I was so happy to see them. I can always remember that my mother looked the same as when I left. Ernie had a new 1953 Chevrolet four-door that he had just bought. It was really a nice one. We drove to a café and went in to eat. Ernie ordered me a steak, but I told him I couldn't eat it. My stomach had shrunk so much, it didn't take much at all to fill it up.

Home Sweet Home

We drove all the way back home. Ernie did the driving. We went through Colorado, but I was glad to get out of the mountains—I'd been looking at them for three years! I was sure glad to get to Kansas. It was good to be able to look across the fields and see a good distance without seeing mountains. Narka had a population of probably 500 people. Mom and the boys had my pictures hanging on the wall just like I had left them. It was so good to be home. I was 180 pounds when I left home, but 119 pounds now. But there wasn't anything wrong with me that Mom's home cooking couldn't cure!

The first night I got home, brother Delbert had a date with a gal, but Mom wouldn't let him go because I just got home. The only brothers at home were Bob, Delbert, and Gary. Bob was going to college in Fairbury, and Delbert and Gary in Narka. Brother Ernie was manager of Gambles in Fairbury, Nebraska. I spent some days with him and went out on the range and shot blue rocks.

The community of Narka and the surrounding towns had a big homecoming dinner for me. There were lots of people there, and I was glad to see them all. They had taken donations and gave me a new 1953 Ford light green four-door. I sure was surprised and happy too. I drove it to church at Hubbell the next day. A guy by the name of Eddie Werth who was in my camp was also there. I met him on the ship coming home. He was from Salina. I had gotten home in time for the Belleville fair—first time I'd ever been to it, even though I had just lived in Narka.

Fort Riley: Honorable Discharge, 1954

In a few weeks, after leave at home, Don reported to Fort Riley. He had several medical checkups. His teeth were in bad shape from the three years in prison camp, but he would not go along with the recommendation by the dentist to have them pulled.

Don re-enlisted for another year, and his mother wasn't happy about it at all. She felt that Don had been through enough, and besides, her sons had served enough for their country. Ernie had had service in World War II, Milt was in both the Army and the Air Force and had served over 20 years, Vern served in the Army, Bob was in the Coast Guard, Delbert in the Marines, and Gary in the Army. The commanding officer called Don into his office one day, and they had a long talk. Don decided he should get out and was honorably discharged. For his service he received the Unit Citation, the Japanese Occupation Medal, the Korean POW Medal, the Korean Service Medal, with three Bronze Stars, the United Nations Service Medal, the National Defense Medal, the Purple Heart, the Combat Infantryman Badge, and the Good Conduct Medal.

A short time after Don got home he married Laura.

Epilogue

For a couple of years after Don was discharged, the CIA sent agents around to see him about POWs who were turncoats or who were suspected to be turncoats. "I finally told them I refused to talk anymore as I was trying to forget the past and get on with a new life," Don said.

Don did just that. Don has now been married to Laura for 41 years. They have two sons, Tim and Jim, and enjoy their three grandchildren, Joe, Nick, and Ryan.

Don has attended several POW conventions over the years. He found out at one of them that the division commander, General Dean, was captured in July at the Kum River. He was housed in a former museum and ate food prepared by a Chinese chef. He slept on a mattress with sheets and could walk 12 miles a day to stay in shape. He was given a tailor-made suit to wear at his release. "His captors knew, of course, that the world press would be present with their cameras to take pictures. It was all for propaganda," Don explained.

Today Don flies the American flag every day. "I do it for the POWs and buddies I knew who died for it."

Point of Interest

Unique for the Korean POWs was the secrecy to which they were sworn, or at least urged to keep, because of postwar collaborational investigations and trials. Such silence for those who needed to talk out their experience was likely a contributing factor in ongoing emotional and psychological disease.

– 11 –

CORPORAL
EDUARDO DEANDA
U.S. ARMY

187th Airborne Combat Team
Captured During a Retreat from Pyongyang
Prisoner of War
November 30, 1950–August 5, 1953
Camp Five

World War II: Soviet and U.S. Agreement

After World War II the Soviet Union and the United States came to an agreement concerning the surrender of the Japanese soldiers. The Soviets agreed to take the Japanese in North Korea, and the United States would take those in the south. The Soviets established a Communist regime, organized a North Korean army, and militarized the 38th parallel. On June 25, 1950, the North Koreans invaded the south.

The United Nations forces entered the war, and, under the direction of General Douglas MacArthur, the American forces and troops of Britain and other commonwealth nations pushed the North Koreans back across the 38th parallel and continued until they had control of Pyongyang, the capital of North Korea. To MacArthur's surprise, his forces were met head-on by 60,000 Chinese troops, beginning in late October. Although Peking had warned that it would enter the war if the UN forces continued, no one took it seriously.

187th Airborne Combat Team: In Korea

In August 1950 the 187th was detached from the 11th Airborne Division at Fort Campbell, Kentucky, for duty in Korea. The first of the unit arrived in

Corporal Eduardo DeAnda

Japan on August 18, 1950, with the rest of the 187th arriving on September 20, 1950.

Four days later, the 3rd Battalion was airlifted to an airfield west of Seoul, Korea, with the mission of securing the airfield prior to the arrival of the rest of the team. At first, the 187th was attached to Y Corps as a general reserve in the Inchon-Seoul area, and it cleared the Kimpo Peninsula. On October 4 the unit was attached to I Corps and was scheduled for deployment in a parachute spearhead capacity above the 38th parallel.

The first combat parachute jump of the war was executed on October 20 into Sukchon and Sunchon areas north of Pyongyang, the North Korean capital. Eduardo DeAnda was one of those airborne soldiers to jump 30 miles into enemy territory and set up a position at Pyongyang.

The Chinese Counterattack: November 30, 1950

An estimated 200,000 Chinese made an attack on the American positions. The under-estimation of Chinese strength forced the American troops to retreat. During the retreat DeAnda was knocked unconscious and left for dead. Six or seven hours later the Koreans came down to pick up weapons left behind by the retreating American troops. By now DeAnda was conscious but bleeding from the head. He spotted the Koreans and began firing his .45 pistol at them. In minutes the Koreans had DeAnda surrounded; the fight was over, and the wounded soldier was captured.

The First Weeks as a Prisoner of War: Pyongyang

The Koreans took DeAnda to a shack in the city and stripped him of his clothing except for fatigue pants and shirt. And then began the hellish 33-month ordeal as a prisoner of war.

Members of the press gather as newly repatriated soldiers exit the ambulance that brought them to Freedom Village, Munsan-Ni, during Operation Big Switch. U.S. Army photo by Private Up Gwin, August 5, 1953.

There were 17 other Americans captured in the area. DeAnda and the other prisoners were kept in Pyongyang for six weeks. Each day they were on work details to clear the roads after the American bombing raids. The work was hard labor, but it was made even worse by the treatment by their captors. The Koreans gave the prisoners no medical attention at all. DeAnda's head wound was infected and needed medical attention, and the prisoners were fed a small portion of buggy rice each day. "The Koreans were very hard on us. We had very little to eat and no medical attention. They would kick us and were very inhumane. We had to survive the best we could," DeAnda explained.

After surviving six weeks in Pyongyang, the prisoners were moved.

The March: To Camp Five

The march from Pyongyang to Camp Five took a month. "We used to march at night and sleep during the day," DeAnda said. Sometimes they would go for days without anything to eat. When they did get food, it was buggy rice that did nothing to take the edge off the hunger pains knotting in the prisoners' stomachs.

The subzero weather took its toll as well. After two weeks of marching, DeAnda's feet froze. He had no feeling in either foot and often fell. Each time he fell, the Koreans would kick him. When he stood, he felt the sharp pain in his back of a rifle butt from a Korean soldier.

During the march through the hills DeAnda saw hundreds of dead bodies stripped naked so that the Koreans could be clothed. Finally, after 30 days of marching, the prisoners arrived at Camp Five. DeAnda and the other 13 prisoners considered themselves lucky they had made it. Three of their fellow soldiers had died on the march. The Koreans threw the dead to the side of the road as if they were hunks of meat and continued the forced march with no emotion.

Camp Five

The camp was the first of the permanent camps. DeAnda estimated that there were 3,000 POWs from Great Britain, Turkey, France, the Philippines, and other United Nations areas. In addition to holding prisoners, it was the Communist headquarters for the entire POW camp system in North Korea.

The camp was surrounded by a four- to five-foot barbed-wire fence. The prisoners were housed in unheated mud huts 10 to 12 per hut.

The living conditions were barbaric. There was no sanitation or medical care, and the food was inadequate—millet seed and buggy rice. Many deaths began to occur. "Many died from contaminated water, dysentery, cholera, and lack of medical care. I caught pneumonia in the spring. They were going to take me to the 'deadhouse,'" DeAnda explained. "Soldiers would die every day, and the bodies were taken to the hills and buried." They buried about 1,400 men that first winter.

"Everyone had lice, worms, and bedbugs. We wore the same clothing month after month" DeAnda recalled. "We tried to eat soap and water to rid our bodies of worms."

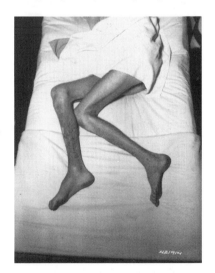

Repatriation: August 5, 1953

On July 27, 1953, the armistice was signed, and released POWs began arriving at Panmunjom about a week later. Operation Big Switch began on August 5, 1953. That was DeAnda's lucky day. After 33 months of captivity he was one of the first to be released. "I thought that I was in good shape," DeAnda said, "compared with how sick I was before." He weighed

The emaciated legs of PFC John L. Robinson, who was captured by the communists in Korea and repatriated under terms of the POW exchange. U.S. Army photo, April 23, 1953.

85 pounds. He had tuberculosis and stomach problems from intestinal worms, and he was covered with lice and bedbugs. He was flown to Japan and then to Brooks Army Hospital in San Antonio, Texas. After several months of recovery DeAnda was honorably discharged from the Army.

Epilogue

On May 4, 1997, Eduardo DeAnda passed away. His wife, Ignacia, said that Eduardo was a good man, husband, father, and grandfather. They all are proud of his patriotism and service to his country. He is sadly missed by them all.

Points of Interest

Unique to the Korean POWs was the endless mental and emotional harassment, humiliation, and brainwashing, called political indoctrination by the Chinese. Hour after hour, day after day, such indoctrination, often coupled with physically and psychologically brutal interrogation, took a measureless toll on the POW's psyche.

The Korean POWs returned to their homes, got married, raised their families, and provided for those families, and usually never asked for anything for their service to their country.

– 12 –

Private First Class Abel Garcia U.S. Army

82nd Anti-Aircraft Automatic
Weapons Self-Propelled Battalion
Captured When His Position
Was Overrun by Chinese Troops
Prisoner of War
December 1, 1950–August 1953
Camp Three and Camp Five

The Draft: Korea, 1949–1950

Abel Garcia was drafted into the Army in January 1949. After six weeks of basic training at Camp Chaffee, Arkansas, he was assigned to Fort Bliss with the 82nd Anti-aircraft Automatic Weapons Self-Propelled Battalion. He was sent to Fort Lewis, Washington, for training. On June 25, 1950, when the North Koreans crossed the 38th parallel, his unit was put on alert. Four days later various units were shipped to Korea. Garcia was sent in August 1950.

Korea: The Counter Offensive, November and December 1950

From August through November 1950 Abel's unit was in support of the 19th and 24th Infantry Regiments during numerous battles in the push north. The UN forces were near the 38th parallel and had pushed the North Korean People's Army north across the 38th parallel. They had set up a defensive position near the 38th parallel.

The last day of November Garcia and members of his unit were sent out

117

to retrieve some quad-50 machine guns mounted on trailers during a retreat of their forces. The guns were blown up so the enemy couldn't use them. At 2:00 A.M. on December 1 everybody stopped, and they were given the order that every man was on his own. They were surrounded by the Chinese army.

Garcia was placing rocks in a makeshift foxhole when the Chinese started up the hill. "They could have just blown us away," Garcia explained. "If they were Koreans they would have shot us. I didn't surrender, I was captured."

The Capture: December 1950

"In most cases the Chinese won't take your clothing, but the Koreans will," Garcia remembered. "Even the underwear." Garcia and the other prisoners were taken to a shack and stripped of their clothing. Then each day they worked clearing the roads after the American bombing raids.

The March: The Mining Camp, Death Valley

After several weeks they started the march.

We moved at night and hid during the day. We stopped first at a mining camp. Men were dying daily from dysentery, pneumonia, and starvation. I was lucky because we were only at the mining camp for four or five days. I think if I had stayed for very long I would have died too.

We continued the march at night. The winter was cold. It was below zero, and I had frostbite. Men were dying as we walked. They were left on the trails for the Koreans to strip them of their clothing. Some prisoners were too weak to continue, and the guards would just shoot them on the spot. They had no concern at all. Just blank looks on their faces as they walked off from the dead bodies.

We arrived at Death Valley about a week later. This camp was more of the same—dysentery, pneumonia, starvation, and death. Prisoners were dying, as many as ten or 12 a day. I kept trying to move around, and it must have helped because many of the prisoners would just give up. If they got dysentery, they would lie down and most of them didn't get back up.

We were at Death Valley for a few days and then started the march again. Finally, after a month, we arrived at Camp Five.

Camp Five

Originally the POW camps were controlled by the North Koreans, but by 1951 they were operated by the Chinese. "The first year the Koreans kept 25–30

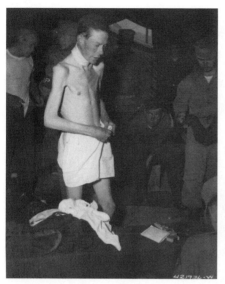 

Left: **Private Reggie Sullivan, captured by the Communists and repatriated under terms of the POW exchange, shows the effects of malnutrition as he takes off his POW clothing for a clean uniform at the 45th Mobile Army Surgical Hospital in Freedom Village, Munsan-Ni. U.S. Army photo, April 1953.** *Right:* **Abel Garcia.**

in a small shack, and those who died during the night were thrown out," Garcia recalled. "The huts were more like freezers. You could see ice and frost on the walls. The Koreans would threaten and torture us, and tell us that by the end of the day we would be dead. They would take us out of the shack, pick up their pistols, walk a short distance, and then bring us back. That was torture. The food was not adequate. We received small portions of millet seed, barley, corn, seaweed, and sometimes rice." Garcia experienced a rapid weight loss. He developed dysentery, intestinal worms, body lice, and bedbugs.

Garcia was assigned to a burial detail one day to bury 50 bodies. The Yalu River was frozen, along with the ground. "I tried to make a hole, but I could not lift the pick."

Camp Three

We had to sit in indoctrination classes every day. It didn't mean anything to me. I ended up being labeled as a reactionary, and after about a year in Camp Five I was sent to Camp Three. It was a hard-labor camp set up for those of us who would not cooperate. This camp was more of the same: dysentery, pneumonia, starvation, and death.

It was self-determination and the will to live that kept me going. I made a promise to myself that I wouldn't let the Communists get the best of me.

Captain Thomas Evers, left, and Major Steven Bettenger look at Major Robert Burns through his long hair and beard—grown while in POW camp—at the Freedom Village, Munsan-Ni, during Operation Day Switch. U.S. Army photo, September 15, 1953.

And they didn't. After 33 months as a prisoner of war the armistice was signed. I knew then that I was going to make it.

Repatriation: August 1950

Garcia was released on August 29, 1953, and after recuperating for several months he returned to the United States in December 1953. After being discharged, he found it difficult to find work. There was a lot of discrimination, and finding jobs was difficult. The only job available for Hispanic Americans was picking cotton. "That didn't make me a traitor," Garcia said proudly.

Epilogue

Today Garcia wears sunglasses and carries a white cane, a carryover from the war when POWs' eyesight deteriorated due to malnutrition.

Points of Interest

The Koreans trace their ancestry back to Central Asian tribes of the steppe and the desert, and so while they physically resemble the Chinese, their language is not at all like that of the Chinese. It is more like Turkish, Japanese, and Mongolian.

Most of the American troops the president ordered into Korea had been stationed in Japan. Their impression was that they were going for a brief "police action" and would be back in Japan in a relaxed atmosphere soon enough. Of the 400 American soldiers in the first combat encounter with the North Koreans, fewer than 250 survived.

– 13 –

SERGEANT
KENNETH F. NEVILL
U.S. MARINE CORPS

7th Marines, 2nd Battalion, F Company,
1st Platoon, 1st Marine Division
Captured When Outpost East Berlin
Was Overrun by the Chinese
Prisoner of War
July 7, 1953–August 23, 1953
Camp Six

Korea: A Shattered Image, 1953

Like many 18-year-old Marines, Ken had fantasies and images of being a Hollywood Marine. That was reinforced by his drill sergeant in boot camp, and in 1953 a lean, mean, gung-ho Sgt. Kenneth Nevill full of Semper Fi arrived in Korea ready for combat duty.

Ken's first experience was a disappointment when he landed in reserve rather than on the front lines of battle. The fight for outposts Reno, Carson, and Vegas was raging. Before the battle was to end, there would be 801 wounded, 116 killed, and 98 missing in action.

Shortly after the battle ended, Ken was ordered to an outpost named East Berlin. It was on a mountain that was small in comparison with the surrounding topography, but its location was such that anyone on it would have a bird's-eye view of the main line of resistance. Obviously this made the position a strategic one.

Ken learned that if the Chinese breached the line and got through his position, they would have a straight shot at the capital of Korea and control of the main supply route to the allied forces to the east, and if that happened it could possibly lengthen the war by months.

Loaded with a field transport pack, personal belongings, ammo, and a Browning automatic rifle (BAR), Ken was exhausted by the time he reached the outpost. But exhausted or not, the only thing Ken was thinking of was to get warm and dry. During the entire walk it poured rain, and Ken was soaked through. His packstraps dug into his shoulders, and he had mud on him from head to toe. Just as it appeared that they had reached their position with a well-earned rest, Ken learned that he had to continue on for another 250 yards out past their lines. When they finally reached the position, they had to use rope, to climb up the wet, slippery slope to reach the trench line. As Ken started up the rope it began to cut his hands. Halfway up he lost all strength, but someone from the trenches came down and helped him to the top.

Ken was glad to be in position but was tormented by the cold and wet conditions. Then he learned that he had the first watch. It was a miserable night, but Ken had a false sense of security because of the steep incline on the mountain. If only he had known how many times the outpost had changed hands and that he was standing above a Chinese tunnel, he would have been much more alert.

The next night Ken stood watch. There was a mist hanging over the mountaintops, and it was dark as sin out in the rice paddies. Every shadow loomed mysteriously in every rice paddy and on every ridge. It was a chilling sight, and Ken tugged at his poncho to gather it in around his shoulders to get what protection it offered. He called softly to Monty, who was supposed to be in the next fighting hole down, and was also the last man on Ken's right. He was Ken's assistant BAR man. In a firefight he was supposed to help protect Ken and furnish extra ammo. Besides his own ammo belt, he carried an ammo belt for the BAR. To Ken's relief, Monty was awake, but little did Ken know that it would be their last communication.

The Battle

The silence of the night was shattered with a deafening blast; one that sent me reeling as flying shrapnel, dirt, and shock waves pelted me, knocking my helmet from my head. Every nerve and fiber in my body reacted violently as a wave of horror swept over me. Reacting instinctively, I jerked at my poncho, yanking it off and letting it fall where it might. Almost in that same instant, there was another blinding flash; an explosion lifted me into the air, then slammed me to the bottom of the trench. Extremely bright lights flashed before my eyes; I felt as if my whole body were being crushed, but for a split second, as shells exploded around me, I felt a strange serenity and heard the voice of my mom telling me, "Son, don't join the Marines, for they are the first to land."

That serenity soon turned back into terror. The stench from the gases of burnt gunpowder burned my nostrils, as I tried desperately to regain my breath. Excruciating pain from the loud ringing in my ears made my head feel like it would explode. I could feel every flash and thunder of exploding shells. Each one sent waves of fear grasping at my soul. Is this what hell is like? Shock waves and flying missiles of steel were zinging all about, killing anything that might be in the way. Dust and gases of spent gunpowder hung in the air like a fog of death, the remainder of death passing me by. My helmet was lying next to me; out of fear and self-preservation, I reached for it, jamming it down on my head. I huddled in terror against the trench and tried to squeeze all my body into the confines of the helmet. The helmet seemed to have shrunk. As the flash and the thunder of shells exploded around me, I was praying to God for deliverance from this hell, for never had I ever experienced so much terror, a terror beyond description and a terror that left me numb, both physically and mentally. When the shelling stopped, I was left in a state of limbo—without feeling of any sort.

As suddenly as the noise had erupted, it became silent, and I grabbed my BAR lying in the trench. It was a deadly silence, a prelude to an approaching enemy, an enemy with but one object in mind—take the hill at any cost. They took the hill, but it would be a costly piece of real estate for them. I was aware of what was about to take place. I had learned at Camp Pendleton during combat training that assault troops are not too far away when the shelling stops. I looked over the side of the trench, expecting to see the enemy. The first movement I saw was to the left and about 20 yards or so down the hill. There I saw the Chinese coming up the slope. I began firing at them, and I called Monty to give a hand, but there was no answer. The hill was aglow from a source of light I have yet, to this day, to be able to explain. It must have been from flares I was unaware of at that time, however. I was acutely aware of everything going on around me, as in a dream, seeing events form, seeing the Chinese come up the hill. I was facing an approaching enemy, and I had no emotions of fear for my own safety. I was sensing my surroundings rather than seeing or feeling them. Shock has that effect on some people in a traumatic situation, and this was a traumatic situation, a matter of killing or being killed.

The Chinese were coming up a small dip along the edge of the cliff. That appeared to be the only way up, and they came through it in a hurry. I began to fire into them, and they fell back like a row of dominoes being knocked over. I could see dark stains of blood appear on some, as my rounds hit the target. As they fell, others would run over them. With the enemy breathing down my neck, changing the magazine in my BAR, came with an uncanny ease of perfection—getting a magazine inserted as fast as I could was not fast enough. The tide of the enemy swept on, and like waves on the beach, there seemed to be no end. This was no probing attack, for there were too many of them—how did they get across the rice paddies so quietly and so quickly? At that moment, I had no feeling of killing other human beings because I had no feelings. Everything seemed that it wasn't really happening at all. There was no past; there was no future; only now. Time had no meaning this night. I was reaching like a machine, subconsciously doing what I had been programmed to do in combat training. I had no power of reasoning or thoughts; if there is such a thing as pure concentration, I must have had it this night for I was reacting to each event as it took place—or was I? Did I doubt my prayers and my belief in God? At that time I did not, but as years passed, I had forgotten. "Yea, though I walk through the valley of the shadow of death, I will fear no evil." Was it fear or faith that sustained me? I have yet to find the answer.

My BAR jammed, and I ducked down to clear it. I could see a loose cartridge causing the hangup. I tried to shake it free, but it wouldn't come out. I removed the trigger housing quickly. I had always had trouble removing the pin that held the housing in place—this time it came out without a hitch. The jammed cartridge fell free when I pulled the bolt back. I put the trigger housing back in, and the next thing I can remember, I was throwing fragmentation grenades at the Chinese.

The Capture

Ken realized that the Chinese were too close for him to expose himself again, for the time that he had used to remove the trigger housing and to reassemble it was to the advantage of the Chinese advancing up the hill. Ken began tossing grenades from a string of them that were hung across his fighting hole, remarkably still intact. He was throwing them as fast as he could, and then as he looked up, a Chinese soldier was pointing a burp gun at him. Ken recalls,

We stared at each other eyeball to eyeball for a split second. He jumped back and I stopped reaching. I started reaching for the grenade again at about the same time he reappeared, and like a swarm of ants on a grasshopper half a dozen Chinese jumped into the trench with me as others moved up the hill. One was tying my hands in front of me with a strip of cloth, while the others searched me, removed my ammo belt, and a pearl-handled dagger I had bought in Japan. Another soldier picked up my BAR. I was led up the hill as the Chinese continued their attack. The only thing was, there was nothing to attack for my faithful comrades had left me and another BAR man named Richards. Richards, from Brooklyn, suffered a compound fracture of his leg from the shelling, and with him down I was the only one defending the outpost. We were the two captured that night.

As I was led up the hill, we came upon a Marine lying face down, his helmet still on his head. I guessed it to be Monty. One of the Chinese soldiers fired a burst into his back, then turned and pointed his burp gun at me. He started walking toward me speaking in a belligerent tone—cursing me, I guess. It was his intention to kill me. I calmly watched him come, knowing what he was going to do, but still I did not have the feelings of fear for my own safety. The Chinese soldier who was leading me up the hill began shouting excitedly in a high-pitched voice and gesturing wildly with his hands toward the soldier coming toward us. Another Chinese, one who must have been an officer, quickly shouted at him in a harsh tone. Whatever he said to him caused the other one to stop. He stood there glaring at me before he went on his way. I was led back down the hill, and we had to go through their dead and wounded to get off the hill. Just a few feet in front of our trench line lay a group of dead Chinese soldiers. They must have bunched up when they reached our lines, and one of my grenades landed smack dab in the middle of them. There was one young dead Chinese soldier looking up at me as we passed. I could have sworn he was alive, but there, placed under his armpit, lay a large black termite grenade and a piece of cloth tripwire leading away from him. I wasn't sure if he was dead or alive, but those eyes seemed to follow me as we passed. I had a feeling of innocence, but yet I knew I must have had some feelings of emotion that night, as I tried to ignore what I had seen. Farther down, more dead Chinese lay where they had fallen. I understood then why that Chinese soldier was so intent on killing me that night, and why, for the next four nights, I was given special attention by the Chinese and their interrogators.

The Beatings and Interrogation: Four Days of Hell

Ken was led down to the base of the hill to the tunnel that went under his outpost. The Chinese had dug the tunnel, and it couldn't be seen from the outpost because of the sudden drop-off. That was how the Chinese had been able to throw so many men at Ken's outpost so quickly. There was a lot of activity around the tunnel entrance, so the Chinese led Ken out across the rice paddies, slipping and sliding on the wet narrow paths toward enemy lines. The sweet fragrance of the night reminded Ken of a freshly cut field of weeds in the country, where he had spent many hours of childhood leisure down by the creek. His sense of that fragrance quickly ended, with a sudden severe pain hitting Ken at the base of his spine. "I knew I was in for a beating," Ken explained.

I fell backward across the narrow levee, ending up in the shallow, cold water of a rice paddy. The two Chinese began kicking me in my sides and back as I rolled over onto my stomach trying to get on my feet. I felt this was as far as I would ever go. My flak jacket absorbed some of the blows, but I was hurting awfully bad. I was sure that I was going to be kicked to death by those two Chinese soldiers. I knew then too that it wasn't a dream. The mental part of me was numb, but the physical part sure wasn't. As I was getting to my feet they stopped kicking me, but I was jerked and shoved forward the rest of the way across the rice paddies. There hadn't been a word uttered by either one of them as they were kicking me. I couldn't see their faces, for it was really dark. I would bet one of them was the one who had wanted to shoot me earlier. I was led onto their trench line and into one of their tunnels, where I was kept under close scrutiny but from a distance, only as far as the length of that tunnel would allow. As I sat there in the dim light, I saw a potato masher grenade leaning up against the side of a tunnel that ran perpendicular to the one I was in. It was wide enough at that junction that I could see a Chinese soldier with the cunning look of a fox ready to jump a chicken sitting a little ways back in the darkness and beside him, within an arm's length, sat his burp gun. It was a setup, and the state of mind I was in, he must have figured I was stupid enough to go for the grenade. There wasn't any way I could have reached that grenade, pulled the cap to the firing mechanism, and thrown it. First off, my hands were tied, and I had never seen a potato masher up close.

I would have been shot before I could reach it. Anyone in his right mind would not have tried going for it. In the state of mind that I was in, it was just an observation without logic or consequence, for nothing registered in my mind. It seemed the only thing to do at the time, but at the same instant I went for it, a vision of my future wife flashed across my mind, stopping me from certain death. It wasn't my time to go, for God surely had a guardian angel with me that night.

A short while before they brought Richards in, our side began to respond with a rocket barrage. The rockets exploding outside the tunnels sounded like drums far away. The Chinese didn't have to fear shelling like we did, because once it started they would scoot into their tunnels. Even a direct hit would not have caused too much damage. A flame thrower at the entrance would have. After things quieted down, I was taken through their narrow tunnel toward the rear. After leaving the impact area, I began estimating distance and guessing at what direction I was being led. If I managed to escape, I wanted to find my way back to our lines. I made a mental note of the location of a mobile anti-aircraft gun we passed. It had been rolled out of a huge opening in the side of a cliff. Other than that and the interrogation stations, that was all the useful information I came upon. There wasn't a sign of life anywhere. At last I was beginning to think and reason logically again, but one thing kept running through my mind over and over again: how would Mom take it when I was reported as missing in action? That worried me, for I knew she had taken it pretty hard when my older brother had drowned.

The Interrogations: Psychological Torture

For the next four days and nights Ken was interrogated, with little sleep. The psychological torture of deprivation of sleep and the lack of food and water were pure hell.

Water was the foremost thing on my mind and what I needed most from the time I was captured. At first, I was given just enough water to keep me going. We had been briefed on the Chinese methods of extracting information from prisoners and were cautioned that any information from prisoners, even seemingly unimportant information, could be of use to the enemy. I was aware that the Chinese already knew what was on our outpost, but when they laid a contour map in front of me and started asking questions about the location of our command posts and other locations of our units I became very illiterate. The fact was, I didn't know exactly where I was, nor did I know the location that I had come from, that is, other than the name of the camp. I figured it was safer to play a little dumb than completely dumb. I didn't think I fooled them, but I knew they could not prove otherwise. One of my interrogators told me, "You are very stubborn," but so what, my mother had been telling me that for years.

I was led through mountain villages, from one interrogation point to another, during the day. Each step was an effort to continue, for one boot I was wearing wasn't mine, and it was a size smaller. At night I would be awakened, and interrogated, and at about the time I would get to sleep—with the fleas having their way with me—I would be awakened, and the interrogation would start all over again—the same old questions but with a different approach. I must have been asked the same questions a dozen different ways. What the Chinese wanted most was the location of our company, our battalion headquarters, and our reserve units. The interrogators had tried their best to cross me up, but I managed to remember everything I told them. It was a good thing because it would have been hell to pay if I had been caught giving a different version from the original. Early in the morning we would start for the next interrogation station, always uphill. I believe the only way a person could go through those Korean mountains was up. There was no such thing as down. I lost track of counting the miles, as I just put one foot in front of another, and at each ridge I would be wishing that it would be the top. As bad as the walking was I hated going through the villages even more. Every village we went through there would be a crowd waiting. How they knew we were coming was beyond me. There was one village where they were really belligerent, while in others they just came out of curiosity. I don't know why that one village was so hostile. I was hit in the forehead with a rock that almost knocked me out. In that village even the guards appeared frightened, for we made a hasty trip through the village, and for the first time those guards weren't strutting like peacocks. How well I remember that. I began to welcome the sight of the interrogation stations—there I could rest. The next two stations proved to be quite different in their approach. At the first of the two I was intimidated with physical torture. I was ushered into a small shed by two Chinese guards, one on each arm. They set me down, while holding my arms as two others removed my boots, almost tearing them off. Another Chinese brought in a pan of hot charcoals and put them near my feet on the dirt floor. The interrogator sitting at a table glared at me and then calmly said, "Warm your feet." My feet weren't cold. They were sore but not cold. The two guards around me released my arms, and stood around me as the head honcho began asking me questions as if the intimidation was never intended. The questions were the same as I had been asked at all the other interrogation stations. However, the addition of the charcoal was new.

After that session, I was fed some tasteless vegetable-looking stuff with little cubes of something in it that looked and tasted like rubber. It was food, I think. Afterward, I was soon started on my way to the next station with my same two guards, but this time they did not bind my hands together. It was much easier walking with my hands free, but still the grade was uphill, and my boot still hadn't stretched any. There was one interrogator who appeared at every interrogation point accessible by road. I don't know if it was by design or coincidence, but on every road we used he would drive by in a big, black, chauffeur-driven car. I thought he looked rather comical sitting there in the back seat in his black uniform. I will say one thing about him: he was persistent and intelligent. He was sharp with interrogation too, because he would engage me in general conversation to get what information that he could. I was aware of that and chose my answers carefully. He was always polite and congenial, but so is a rattlesnake at a distance. He never asked questions directly concerning my unit, but tried to lead me in the direction of when I first entered the Marines to the time before my capture. The last time I saw him was at a village along the way where he had stopped to eat. He would spend at least an hour talking with me, but always in the presence of an armed guard. They must have thought I was a dangerous person. Always in the back of my mind was the caution at the briefings, "Any seemingly unimportant information could be useful to the enemy. Only give your name, rank, serial number, and where you were born." The latter is great for someone sitting behind a desk making up those guidelines, but in reality it could and probably did cost the lives of many who adhered to it. It's best, in my opinion, to tell an enemy what he already knows, than to clam up completely, for there is no way they can know what you know.

If one chooses to go that route, it is in his own best interest to remember what has been said. I think that now is the general consensus among the elite of our military and some other intelligence branches. Going back to my first interrogation, I knew I was in trouble there. At that first interrogation, which was about a mile from the lines, there were several older Chinese soldiers sitting before me, staring at me with a stern look. I think they were line officers, by the way my guards acted. It reminded me of a court of inquiry, and when I quoted the Geneva Convention agreement concerning POWs they took my Geneva Convention card away from me. China was one of the countries that did not sign that agreement. I would never have made it past that first interrogation point had I continued to follow those guidelines of giving my name, rank, serial number, and where I was born. When they took my

Geneva Convention card, I realized that I had better start saying something. I am sure that action saved my life; however, I still had reservations about doing any talking. I have no doubt that I made the right decision. Going back to the third day of my captivity, I recall that we came to what looked like a ridge—I was still praying for a change of direction, namely, downhill. The boot that was too small was giving me fits; I had put my boots on in the dark when I was awakened for a midnight watch. I had picked up the wrong boot and was only half awake and didn't notice the difference at the time. Each step was painful, and when I faltered any at all, I got a burp gun in the back. The top of the ridge was flat and lined with trees, but to my great disappointment the other side was upward. Always upward. We came to a building that blended in with the surrounding area. The building projected out from a cliff but was hidden by the line of trees. This quaint-looking station had a intriguing mystique about it, something that at some other time or place would be relaxing to just sit and look at. Inside the shed the furnishings were the same—a straight-back chair sitting behind a bare table, with another chair against the wall. I was ushered in and stood before the table. My two guards were relieved by two others. After a long wait standing before the table, a Chinese in a dark uniform that looked more like pajamas came in, sat down, and laid some papers on the table. He stared at me as he said something in Chinese. Then one of the guards moved the chair behind me. I was told to sit. He immediately began to tell me I had better cooperate with him or there would be grave consequences. This slant-eyed fellow reminded me of a snake coiled and ready to strike, but I had no intention of changing my story. He asked basically the same questions, and I gave him the same answers. He jumped to his feet, very agitated, and said, "You will tell me what I ask. You will be truthful!" I told him that I was being truthful, and besides I didn't have to tell him anything but my name, rank, serial number, and where I was born. That really made him mad. He came tearing around the table speaking Chinese in a harsh tone. He grabbed the back of my chair, jerked me away from the table, and at the same time knocked me out of the chair onto a dirt floor. The two guards grabbed me and pulled me up to my knees. The next thing I knew there was a pistol pushing against my temple. He said something to me in Chinese and then said in English, "You have one minute to pray to your God." I was held there, and all I could do was stare at the dirt floor. I must have been petrified, for I had no thoughts, only the sense of what was happening. It must have been the terrible fear of death because I experienced the same state of mind that I had on the outpost. I felt the click of the hammer as it was cocked, and every nerve in my body tensed. Then the sharp sound as the hammer snapped to. That sound was like the string of a violin reverberating loudly in an echo chamber—a sound that I have never forgotten. I was lifted on the chair, but the questions after that had no meaning and I remained in a numb silence. I was finally taken into a tunnel that ended several yards into the cliff, given a little candle, and then

I was left alone. I sat there for some time just staring into the darkness of the tunnel as the candle flickered light off the wall of the tunnel. The tunnel began to take shape, and I noticed that the floor was covered with straw. I took pieces of the straw and fashioned a small cross, kneeled before it, and prayed. I made some promises to God. I remembered my childhood and the events leading to my enlistment in the Marine Corps. I wondered if I had been reported missing yet. I knew it was going to be a shock to Mom and I felt sorry for her and the grief she would have. After the candle burned out, I fell into a fitful sleep, half awakened and half asleep. Finally I slept. I was awakened by sounds of a foreign language, and it frightened me. I didn't know where I was for a moment. I thought I was in my bunker and Chinese were outside it. For the first time in three days a normal fear came over me, but it passed when I realized where I was and what was happening. I remembered the evening before, and a cold shiver came over me. Three Chinese came into the tunnel. One was carrying a candle. He gave me a small bowl of food, and the other guard gave me a small bowl of tea. The third guard was carrying a burp gun. They watched me eat the strange tasteless food, and when I finished, the Chinese guard with the candle motioned for me to go with him. I was marched on to another interrogation station and more questioning. This time I didn't open my mouth. I just sat and glared at the interrogator, for now I didn't give a damn. What else could they do to me? I was questioned for a very short period when the interrogator finally accepted that I wasn't going to talk to him. Soon afterward I was led away by the two guards. Late on the fourth day of my capture I was led downhill for the first time. We crossed a shallow flowing stream, not bothering to avoid getting our feet wet. Up a ways I saw a farmhouse. It was used as a gathering station where POWs were kept until there were enough to ship on to POW camps farther north. It was built on a gentle slope surrounded by trees. It was a well-built house, as far as Korean houses go. In the winter it was heated by brick or clay ducts running under the floor. There was a small garden to one side, with a combination chicken house and outhouse. Water was taken from the stream about 50 yards away. The laundry was also at the stream. Closer to the house was another chicken-wire enclosure used as a cage for POWs. The first few minutes there I got to sleep inside the house, but when they started bringing in more POWs we were rotated to the chicken-wire pen. A straw mat served as a bed. At the house I met an Australian and a French Canadian POW. The Australian, named Carl, was a ranch hand in civilian life. The Canadian was from Quebec. Neither one of us could pronounce his name, so we called him Frenchie. They were the first friendlies that I had talked to since my capture. We exchanged events leading up to our capture and the interrogations that we went through. Carl had a rim of a potato masher grenade sticking out between his eye and nose, and during his interrogation he pretended to be crazy, as he put it. He had convinced the Chinese that he was dimwitted, and they didn't interrogate any further. The

Former prisoner of war Nevill is greeted by Brigadier General Joseph C. Burger at Freedom Village.

Chinese couldn't understand Frenchie, with his accent of French and English. I couldn't understand how they gave up so quickly.

Life at the Farm: July 10–27, 1953

Ken remained at the farmhouse for 17 days. Life wasn't too bad compared with the four days of marching and interrogation that Ken had gone through. They were fed twice a day and had an endless supply of water. There was no interrogation, and the prisoners settled into a routine of talking of home, friends, loved ones, and what they would do when the war ended.

A few days later several U.S. Army men were brought into the camp. One had a hard time moving around because he had steel fragments in his buttocks from a grenade that had exploded near him.

A couple weeks later four more prisoners were brought in. They were Marines from G Company of Ken's regiment, and Ken found out that they had been captured at the same outpost where he had been. Ken asked about his unit, but all he got were rumors and excuses from the Marines for how they were captured. Ken took it that they had been captured because they had let their guard down and were simply trying to make excuses for it.

Each day more prisoners were brought in, and the farmhouse became very crowded. As a result, the prisoners were cut to one ration a day. Ken and the rest of the POWs kept busy washing clothes, staying out of the open because of concern that their own fighter planes would not be able to tell the difference between them and the Chinese or North Koreans. The rest of the time was spent talking about the end of the war.

Freedom at Last: July–August 1953

Talking about the end of the war became a reality for Ken and the others on July 27, 1953, the day the truce was signed. Ken and the other prisoners were moved to Camp Six, located northeast of Kaesong.

In August 1953 Ken arrived at Freedom Village, where he received food, medical care, a chance to visit with friends, and, finally, a ship back to the United States.

Nightmares of War

The seven weeks that Ken spent in the POW camp seemed like a breeze compared with experiences of other prisoners who spent much more time and lived through much more hardship. How wrong he was, though, because for 29 years after the war Ken lived a tormented life of shame, depression, anxiety, guilt, and diminished self-esteem. Ken suspected it was from the war, but the most foolish thing that he did was to try to ignore it.

For three decades Ken had relied on rumors from uninformed sources concerning the evidence in Korea, and the end result was a loss of trust, an inability to communicate openly, and a diminished sense of personal dignity. A stepping stone for Ken was psychotherapy at the VA hospital in Dallas where he learned that all things may not be what they seem.

Then Ken had another stroke of luck. One day, while in a bookstore, he picked up a book on the clearance rack entitled, *The U.S. Marine Story.* As he thumbed through it, to his surprise he found that many of the battles that he had been associated with were in the book. Not only that, but the battle of Outpost Little Berlin was in it. It even listed his name as one of the men who had been captured. "All those years I had believed from rumors that most of my company had been killed that morning, trying to retake the outpost.

Recently repatriated PFC Kenneth Nevill eats ice cream during his stopover at Freedom Village.

Kenneth Nevill

It was my platoon and the 2nd Platoon that retook the hill. It's ironic that some of the first ones killed were the ones who had been the defenders, who had left the outpost when the shelling started. The facts were that half of my platoon died trying to retake the outpost. There were 140 wounded by the time the 2nd Platoon retook the hill at 12:33 P.M. that day." Knowing the real facts changed Ken's view.

Going through group therapy, knowing the facts, and writing about his experiences while attending college, Ken began to have a more analytic view of life. Although his capture is still the most vivid moment in his life, after 30 years Ken has begun to heal.

A Point of Interest

By the end of the bloody stand at Pusan and the victory at Inchon and Seoul, it was clear to most Americans that this agony in Korea was no mere police action. Retaking enemy territory, U.S. troops found captives who were horribly mutilated, burned, and castrated.

– 14 –

CORPORAL
BUFORD J. MCNAMERA
U.S. ARMY

24th Infantry Regiment
Captured at Anju When His Unit
Was Surrounded by Chinese Troops
Prisoner of War
November 4, 1950–August 23, 1953
Mining Camp, Camps One, Three, Four, Five, and Nine

The Beginning: Army Life, 1949

Fresh from his family farm near Memphis, Buford McNamera enlisted in the U.S. Army at the age of 17. The six-foot, one-inch, 200-pound farm boy adapted well to Army life and had taken well to engineer training at Fort Belvoir. Buford felt that Army life would provide security, and he married his girlfriend, Theresa, in December.

Six months had passed and the McNameras were expecting their first baby. Then, on June 25, 1950, the unexpected invasion of South Korea hit the headlines. One month later, Buford, an infantryman, received orders for Korea.

Pusan: The Push North, September 1950

Buford arrived in Korea and was immediately assigned to the 24th Infantry Division. The UN forces had taken a defensive position at Pusan. On September 16, 1950, the Eighth Army, including the 19th Infantry Regiment and 24th Infantry Regiment, launched an offensive to coincide with General Douglas MacArthur's amphibious landing at Inchon Harbor behind the Communists. Within three weeks the North Koreans had been driven back across the 38th parallel. Then, as the UN forces scurried closer to the Yalu River between North Korea and Manchuria, the Chinese counterattacked. In early November, Buford and the men in his outfit found themselves facing veteran Chinese soldiers just north of the Chongchon River near Anju on the western coast of North Korea. Buford had been in Korea for four months and had fought many battles. He had been wounded once, on September 17, 1950, and had a Purple Heart to show for it. But this battle would be different. It would be a battle that would affect Buford for the rest of his life.

The Counterattack

Our regiment had moved north of the Chongchon River on November 3 to help defend bridges and tank fords vital to the UN offensive drive. During the day thousands of disciplined, well-trained Chinese troops had worked through low-lying wooded areas and gotten behind us.

Our company had been at an outpost some distance away from the regimental command post. That night, I watched as straggler after straggler, fortunate survivors of a deadly game of cat-and-mouse with the Chinese, withdrew through our outpost to the rear. Then, in the early morning hours of November 4, the frantic order came to withdraw from the outpost and return to the CP, which was being overrun. It was too late.

The Chinese attack, with blaring bugles and whistles screeching, unnerved me because I knew the sound signaled another attack.

I tightened my grip on the Browning automatic rifle (BAR) and strained to see any revealing movement by the enemy as darkness lifted. The sun gradually illuminated the landscape, and the hopelessness of the situation was all too clear. There were two platoons of us, about 100 men, all battle weary, short on ammunition, and we were cut off from the battalion on top of a windswept hill surrounded by the Red Chinese army.

I didn't have time for despair, I simply reacted. I fired round after round into the Chinese. They covered the hillside like ants on a mound. I had fought in many skirmishes, but I had never seen anything like this.

The Chinese advanced up the hill in waves, charging upright in full daylight. They wore quilted cotton uniforms, fur boots, and fleece-lined caps. They were well equipped with carbines, grenades, and machine guns.

Masters of camouflage and night movement, the Reds relied upon speed and their favorite battle tactic, "hachi shiki," a V-type ambush, to overrun and cut off the Americans' escape route.

As the day wore on, I was fatigued and weary. Smoke covered the area, and my eyes burned from smoke and sweat. In a brief gap between attacks I gained some strength from thinking about Theresa and wondered if I would ever see her again.

By late afternoon, only eight of us were alive out of the 100 we started with. We were almost out of ammunition. The eight of us decided the best chance of escape was to split up.

The Capture: November 4, 1950

I got into a gully, and crawled about ten yards. I heard a commotion and looked up and saw five or six Chinese. One was armed with a burp gun and one had a British Sten—and that's all I needed to see. I had two .45 caliber pistols, which I threw away. That got them a little excited. I thought for a moment I was going to get it ... but I didn't.

At that time I didn't know if anyone else had made it or been captured. I was interrogated by an English-speaking Red, who at first refused to believe there were no more Americans holding out on the hill. "None but the dead," I told them.

I was taken to what used to be the CP. My platoon sergeant, company commander, and about 60 other prisoners were there. Then in a short time we started the long march to the rear.

The March

We marched through the snow for three weeks to a mining camp known as Death Valley on the way to the Yalu. There they turned us over to the North Koreans. They took our boots and every other thing of value ... wallets, cigarettes, lighters, watches, pencils.

Then the Chinese made us walk farther north, barefoot, to Camp Five on the Yalu. Rags were used for footwear, and I got severe frostbite to my feet and almost lost my toes.

The Winter of 1950. The winter of 1950 was one of the most severe recorded in history. From 45 to 58 people died per night that winter in Camp Five. With morning came the horrible task of burying the dead in frozen ground. The camp soon had a new name—Death Camp.

An American doctor was among the prisoners, but he couldn't give us adequate medical care because there were no medical supplies. Men simply starved to death.

I dropped from 208 to below 150 pounds. I was moved to the death compound because the Chinese thought I was going to die. Dysentery, yellow fever, and malaria took a toll, but another prisoner gave me some of his food and dragged me around until I got some of my strength back. Many men got sick and did not want to eat, or could not hold food down, but if you missed a single meal, it'd knock you down. The truth is you had to steal to survive. You could not live on what they gave you.

Food consisted of a red barley mixture soaked in water. It'd swell and

DEPARTMENT OF THE ARMY
OFFICE OF THE ADJUTANT GENERAL
WASHINGTON 25, D. C.

IN REPLY REFER TO

AGPS-D 201 McNamara, Buford J.   5 November 1952
RA 14 324 817 (5 Nov 52)

Mrs. Edith S. McNamara

Lucy, Tennessee

Dear Mrs. McNamara:

    I am writing you concerning your son, Corporal Buford J. McNamara,
who was reported missing in action in Korea on 4 November 1950.

    The Department of the Army has completed a review of all the
known facts and circumstances relative to the whereabouts of your
loved one. In view of the receipt of mail which appears to have been
written by him while in the custody of the opposing forces, and the
release of his name by those forces as an alleged prisoner, an
official determination has been made that he is in a status of
"captured."

    This change in status should not be construed as an official
assurance of his present whereabouts or condition. However, everything
possible is being done to ascertain the condition of our personnel who
have been captured and to secure their release.

    I should like to add that the above mentioned action by this
office will not result in any change in benefits provided by Public
Law 490, 77th Congress, as amended.

    I share personally your anxiety for his early return.

                     Sincerely yours,

3 Incls
    1. Ltr 25 Oct 50 w/env   WM. E. BERGIN
    2. Ltr 24 Dec & Xmas greeting   Major General, USA
       w/env   The Adjutant General of the Army
    3. Ltr 8 Mar 52

Corporal Buford McNamera

fill you up. Rice was a rarity; for Chinese, rice was like steak or turkey for
an American.

    Brainwashing. Some of the Chinese who spoke English tried to tell
us bad things about the United States. I laughed at them because they didn't
know what they were talking about because very few of them had ever been
to the United States.

I stubbornly resisted brainwashing and psychological torture. They told me they would like to kill me, but couldn't because they had a hands-off policy. I know of several cases where prisoners were strung up with ropes and hung from rafters, but it never happened to me. The Chinese talked about American imperialism and made us attend indoctrination classes every day, where English-speaking instructors would try to get us to talk about Communism. They'd try to prove to us how good Communism was. They'd get you down real low and weak, and you'd grasp at anything. But most of us resisted.

They took 163 of us hopeless reactionaries and made a hard labor camp out of us. From dawn till dusk we would chop trees, unload supplies from Chinese junks on the Yalu River, and bust rocks with a sledgehammer.

We leveled off a mountainside and built our own barracks. They split us into three groups—whites, blacks, and Englishmen—and they tried to get us to fight among ourselves. But we stuck together and that made them mad.

Missing in Action: Letters Home, the Reactionary Status. After Buford was captured on the evening of November 4, his unit reorganized with what was left and again fought hard through the night and into the next day until the early morning of November 6, when the Chinese were forced to withdraw with heavy losses. One battalion's official records illustrated the terrible toll, reporting that 474 enemy dead surrounded a single hill, with indications that many more had already been buried.

When the battalion reached the top of the hill where Buford and the other seven men had fought off the Chinese, they found that the men were gone. Buford's wife was notified that he was missing in action.

Because Buford was labeled as a reactionary, his letters home were not mailed out for over a year. It was 13 months before Theresa got an unexpected Christmas present. On December 18, 1951, she was told he was a prisoner of war.

His mail finally began to arrive home. He knew his mail was heavily censored, so when he finally got the chance, he tricked the Chinese by writing that they were feeding him as "good as his baby back home." His

Corporal Buford McNamera

family understood his message, that he was not eating too well, because "Baby" was the family milk cow's name.

The War Is Over: Freedom Village, July 27, 1953

On July 27, 1953, the armistice was signed and the war was officially over. The prisoners were gathered and told that the war had ended. "I really didn't believe it when they said it was over," Buford recalls.

> But when the Red Cross came in and they gave a big feed, the first we'd ever seen ... I knew it was real.
>
> We were taken to Freedom Village, near Panmunjom, where they fed us. Actually, they tried to let us get used to eating American food again. And they wanted to get us stabilized.
>
> I cannot begin to describe the way I felt. When I saw all those American flags, I knew that I was a free man and would make it home.
>
> I learned while I was in the village that I had been promoted to sergeant. I received a letter signed by all 66 inhabitants of my hometown in Tennessee.

A Boat Ride to the States: A Reunion with a Son He Had Never Seen

Onboard ship bound for America, Buford received long overdue medical treatment. In a matter of days he was in the States and then on an airstrip in Memphis.

> I was the last one to get off the plane because I never expected so many people to be waiting. I guess I was nervous or a little embarrassed by all the attention, and then things have happened so fast.
>
> You're gone from home more than three years, and all but five months of that time was spent as a prisoner of the Communists. And while you're gone your wife gives birth to your first child—a son. Much of that time, your family doesn't know whether you are dead or alive.
>
> Then comes a day when you step off a plane, and standing there are your wife, your mother, your sister. And your son. Your mother is holding your son. Your wife runs up the steps and throws her arms around you. You smile into her moist eyes. Then you embrace again. You don't have to explain how you feel. You don't have to. It shows all over.

At the airport, three-year-old Danny had little to say. But once he was home he went charging through the house yelling, "Daddy, Daddy!" Buford took pleasure in taking time to inspect Danny's red car and teddy bear. He was also proud to see his son so excited to see Daddy.

Buford visited with his mother and father, and then he and Theresa went on a second honeymoon at an undisclosed location.

A Military Career, Civilian Life

Buford stayed on active duty in the Army until 1972, when he retired as a chief warrant officer. He was hired by Memphis District in 1973 as an electronic technician and worked as an electronic mechanic at Ensley engineer yard.

Today: A Veteran Leader

Buford is a leader in the community of veterans. During his free time he works with veterans' organizations, such as the VFW, and has served on the board of directors for the Mid-South Chapter of Ex–POWs

"You never realize what freedom is until you become a prisoner," Buford explained. "I never lost the feeling that I was fighting for a good cause. You couldn't pay me a million dollars to do it over again, but I wouldn't take a million dollars for the experience."

– 15 –

PRIVATE FIRST CLASS
CHARLES QUIRING
U.S. MARINE CORPS

I Company, 3rd Battalion, 5th Marines, 1st Marine Division
Captured During a Battle at the Chosin Reservoir
Prisoner of War
December 2, 1950–May 25, 1951
Camp Located at Kangdong—
Camp Eight Was Assigned Kangdong

High School, College, and the Marine Corps: May 1947–August 1948

Charles graduated from high school in Wichita, Kansas, in 1947. He then began his college career at Friends University in Wichita. He completed one year there but was lonely and financially burdened. Charles was looking for a change and enlisted in the U.S. Marine Corps on August 16, 1948. A few days later he arrived at the Marine Corps recruit depot in San Diego, California. For the next eight weeks he spent many days on the grinder (the parade field) in close-order drill, on the obstacle courses, in hand-to-hand combat training, being yelled at by DIs and double-timing everywhere he went. If there had been any doubt in his mind about a change in his life, those doubts were gone by graduation day from boot camp. Charles had just completed the most rigorous challenge of his life—Marine Corps boot camp.

The War Breaks Out: June 1950

After boot camp Charles was stationed at the Marine barracks, Hunter's Point Naval Shipyard, in San Francisco, California. Charles mainly did guard duty on the base, and for the next several months, when he wasn't on duty, he enjoyed the sights of the San Francisco Bay area.

On June 25, 1950, Charles' day was jolted with the news that war had broken out in Korea. In the next few weeks, however, concerns about major war began to diminish as the president declared that this event was a police action. The rumor was that the police action would last for only a short time, but the rumor was soon in conflict with military maneuver. In August 1950 Charles was shipped to Camp Pendleton, where combat units were being formed, supplied with combat gear, and briefly combat trained. Charles managed to get some leave and returned to Kansas to marry his girlfriend, Doris. Then he returned to Camp Pendleton. His new unit was I Company, 3rd Battalion, 5th Marines, of the 1st Marine Division. Two weeks later the newlywed was on his way to Korea.

Korea: 5th Marines–July-November 1950

The 5th Marines became part of the 1st Marine Provisional Brigade. The brigade consisted of the 5th Marines and Marine Aircraft Group 33. The unit sailed for Pusan, Korea, on July 14, 1950, and reached its destination on August 2, 1950. The unit constituted the first land forces sent to Korea from the United States.

A few days after arrival the unit engaged in combat near Changwon. Over the next two weeks the 5th Marines was in combat in Kosong, Chindongni, and Naktong. Toward the end of August they moved back to an area called the "Bean Patch," where they received replacements, rested, and trained in a large beanfield.

In the first part of September the bridge arrived at Pusan and began preparations for landing on Inchon. Charles joined the unit at this time. On September 14, 1950, the unit landed at Pusan, and on September 15 the 5th Marines assaulted and took Cemetery Hill and Observation Hill. Charles was out of action for a couple of weeks with a shrapnel wound.

After recuperating from his wounds, Charles rejoined his unit at Kimpo airfield. The unit moved north, running into a little resistance from the Chinese. A short time later they were relieved by the Army and moved to Wonson. The unit patrolled the east coast with little action.

The Chosin Reservoir: Thanksgiving Day, 1950

On Thanksgiving day the unit was moved up to the Chosin Reservoir in order to seize the vital town of Kyomuli-li. The 5th Marines moved up the east side of the reservoir, where within a few days they were surrounded by the Chinese army. General Lewis Puller was in charge of the Marine units. After assessing the situation, he said, "They are on our left, they are on our right, they are in front of us and behind us; they can't get away from us now."

The Battle: November 25–December 2, 1950

"We had been caught in the trap by the Chinese in late November," Charles explained.

> We were trying to fight our way out to reach Hagaru-Ri and Koto-Ri. On December 1 we were pulling out of the Chosin area, knowing we had to fight our way out. There were massive air drops of rations and ammunition. Most of this was piled up and destroyed by bulldozers. All of us who could walk did so, and the wounded and those with severe frostbite were loaded on trucks and jeeps. We then began our march south.
>
> Our company deployed on a hill that evening. At that time we were down to about two platoons. That night we were attacked by a large number of Chinese soldiers. Another Marine by the name of Ed Wilkins and I shared a small foxhole, which was about two feet deep. The attack consisted of wave after wave of Chinese, accompanied by shouting, whistling, and bugle blasts. We could see them pretty well because of our flares. It seemed that they never ended.
>
> I don't know how long the battle lasted, but it was finally quiet. The Chinese almost always attack at night, so we thought if we could hold out until dawn we would be okay. However, that was not the case. When it began to get light we could see that we were the only Marines on that hill. The rest of our company had pulled out sometime during the night. The only other ones on that hill were the Chinese busily picking up what was left behind.

The Capture

> We thought that if we played dead they might leave us alone. A couple of Chinese came over and nudged us with rifles, but we did not move. We could hear their chatter, and finally a shot was fired. I thought that they had killed Wilkins and I would be next. What they did was let off a round to see if we would react. Finally they reached down and pulled us out of the foxhole and took our weapons.
>
> We were taken to the bottom of the hill where there were many soldiers, some wounded and very angry. It was fortunate that we were taken prisoner, because shortly after we came down the hill our planes flew over, strafing the hill and covering it with napalm.

The Early Days of Capture

"We were taken to a Korean hut where there were several other prisoners," Charles said.

After a few days we were marched to another location where there were several officers and two British Marines. There were 30 of us there, and they allowed us to write a letter attesting to our welfare and more importantly to let our families know we were alive. This information was published in a January 1951 *Los Angeles Times* newspaper. That was the first that my wife knew I was missing. It took several days for Washington officially to notify my wife of my MIA status, but they would not confirm that I was a POW.

The day after we wrote the letters the Chinese brought us all outside and told us we were liberated. Looking around we could not see any of our forces, only the Chinese. They went on to explain that we had been "liberated from the warmongering Wall Street capitalists." This was our first taste of Communist indoctrination. At the time it all seemed like a joke because we had no idea what they were talking about.

The March

After a few days the POWs started moving north. They marched at night across roads frozen solid. "It was difficult for us to walk because of the type of boots we had," Charles explained.

During these marches we would fall down many times. However, the guards were very patient with us and even helped us up. Finally, we learned to shuffle rather than to take steps. Most of the Chinese wore sneakers so they didn't have this problem. One night we rode in open gondola-type cars on a train. Other than that time we walked.

The Prison Camp: December 26, 1950–April 2, 1951

On December 26, 1950, the POWs reached a prison camp at Kangdong, Korea, about 20 miles south of the Yalu River and Manchuria. "This would be our home for the next three months," Charles said.

Unfortunately, we had missed the Christmas party given on Christmas Eve.

There was no fencing of any kind, with only token guards, usually only one or two. We were broken up in squads. The largest group was housed some distance away, and I do not know how they were divided up. In our area there were two squads of enlisted men and one squad of officers. The total camp had about 300 POWs. Our squad had about 15.

Our squad was housed in a small hut. It was only large enough so that the 15 of us could lie down in two rows, head to feet. The walls were plaster, concrete, or mud and always covered with frost. We had straw on the

Compound #3, POW Camp #8, showing (foreground) the latrine and outside urinal and (background) the recreation area and kitchen. U.S. Army photo, May 28, 1953.

floor and the close quarters helped keep us from freezing. Tunnels were under the floor, so that fires could be built to warm the hut. We were not allowed to build fires for fear by the Chinese that our planes would spot us.

One of the most irritating problems was body lice. Most of us wore thermal underwear, and the lice would bury themselves in the folds and creases; then when they warmed up at night they would begin crawling. This would be a chore to remove the underwear and kill all the lice by squeezing them between our fingernails. A few times we were allowed to burn the straw inside the hut, which helped to defrost the walls and also get rid of the body lice for a while.

Food. From the poor diet in prison camp Charles developed dysentery and quickly dropped about 50 pounds. "The type and quantity of food were not enough to sustain a body even without physical activity," Charles said.

We had two meals per day. The basic food was a boiled grain, probably sorghum seed. For the 15 we would get a two-and-one-half-gallon pail at each meal. It was filling but not lasting. In addition we would also get a "side dish." This was usually boiled bean sprouts. Sometimes other things might be added, such as bean curd or some small pieces of meat that appeared to be pork. The meat was suspect since at times we would see a dog skin tacked on a wall to dry. Also, once in a while we would find fishheads, eyes and all. On special occasions, such as Chinese New Year, we would be treated to white rice.

The sorghum seed would be cooked in large cast-iron pots over wood fires. The grain that stuck to the side would be almost like bread if you used your imagination, and usually we would get cooks to scrape it off the pot for us.

At each meal we would also get a pail of boiling water. It reminded some of the guys of being home drinking their morning coffee. All of the water had to be boiled because the Chinese feared bacterial contamination. They would not let us drink water from even fast-running streams or waterfalls.

Medical Treatment. The medical treatment was almost nonexistent. Most of the prisoners suffered from frostbite, colds, and dysentery. "They gave us a small brown pill for the dysentery, but I don't know if it helped," Charles explained.

I saw one Marine with a .45 slug in his leg from a burp gun at the time of his capture. The slug was embedded in his thigh. It was giving him a lot of trouble and pain, so one of the Chinese medics lanced the wound and removed the slug. The only medication they had for it was sulfa powder. The wound never healed.

Any other problems went unattended. We had to rely on our bodies to heal themselves as best they could.

Indoctrination. "The indoctrination was simple and straightforward," Charles explained.

We were taken one at a time to talk to an officer. The only military questions they asked us were concerning the military makeup of the units—the number in each unit and the type of weapons each unit had. This information could be obtained from any military manual. I think they were only testing our honesty. What they were really interested in was the life we had back home. Such things as the jobs our family members held, how much money they made, kind of cars they owned, and homes they lived in. In other words the economic makeup of our families.

At least once a week, sometimes more, we would be taken to a barn where we had to listen to lectures. These would last two or three hours since they were always delivered in both Chinese and English. Examples of lecture subjects: "Who Is the Aggressor in Korea?" "Why Do the Chinese Love Peace?" "Why Is the U.S. the Aggressor?" Other lectures would denounce MacArthur, Truman, Dulles, Rhee, etc. The main theme in all their lectures was that they did not blame us for being in Korea because we had been duped by our "aggressive, capitalist, warmongering leaders"—as if we had a choice

Private First Class Charles Quiring

of being there. After the lecture we would go back to our hut with a Chinese officer and discuss what we had learned.

We were given reading material such as the *Shanghai News*, *Peping Daily News*, *China Review*, etc. After having read these we would have discussions among ourselves and with their officer.

We were also urged to write articles for the camp newspaper, *New Life*. They were printed on very thin paper—probably rice paper—and most were used to roll cigarettes or for toilet paper.

We were taught a song to the tune of "Glory, Glory, Hallelujah": Proletariat forever, Proletariat forever, Proletariat forever. For the party makes us free, *Hey, Hey, Hey*. Then we would sing the same song substituting *solidarity* for *proletariat*. The irony in this was, most of us didn't have a clue about what these terms meant.

In all of this they did now want us to be "yes men." They wanted the opportunity to "clear our minds" and to see their way of thinking. Most of us went along with this charade and were termed "progressive students."

On March 21 they told us some would be sent home to continue the struggle against oppression. They selected 60 of us and played a mind game with us. They would say, "Who will go home and who will stay?" This went on for some time until they chose 20 who would be sent home. The rest would go back to camp. The one Marine who had had the .45 slug removed was included with us, but his wound was giving him too much trouble and he couldn't go with us. This left 19 to be sent home—18 Marines and a Nisei Army interpreter.

Repatriation: April 3, 1951

"I'm not sure about the time we were split from the group of 60," Charles explained.

I think the whole group of 60 started moving south on April 3. We were moved sometimes by truck and other times we walked. One of the prisoners died during the move, and we had to bury him. He wasn't part of the original group, but I think if he had survived he would have been released with us. We continued to move for about three weeks. On May 1, the 19 of us split from the others. We were not told why the other prisoners would not be released, but on May 18 we were told that we were going to be released. Several times we were taken near our lines, only to be pulled back because of increased fighting.

On May 24 we were close enough to our lines that our guards left us to make our way back. This was not so easy since there were Chinese troops moving through our area all night. Hiding out in a nearby hut, we waited until morning to make contact. We stripped wallpaper from the walls of the hut and laid it out in a field—"POW HERE"—and used shell casings to spell out "RESCUE." A spotter plane saw the message, and tanks from the 7th Division came to pick us up. We were evacuated from Chunchon to 1st Marine Division Headquarters. We were finally free. After about three weeks in a hospital in Japan we were sent home.

Life After: 1951–1955

When Charles returned home he was stationed at the Naval Ammunition Depot, McAlester, Oklahoma. His enlistment was up in September 1952. He and Doris had their first daughter, Serena, born on September 6, 1952. He received an honorable discharge and returned to Friends University, Wichita, and received his B.A. in chemistry in May 1955.

Epilogue

After graduating from Friends University, Charles went to work for Mobil Oil Company as a chemist and was with them in Joliet, Illinois, and Augusta, Kansas, until he retired in April 1987. He later worked for Coastal Oil and retired in 1993. He and Doris have three daughters and a son, all married. They enjoy their children, and their ten grandchildren as well.

– 16 –

SERGEANT
WILFRED RUFF
U.S. ARMY

D Company, 38th Regiment, 2nd Division
Captured During a Seek-and-Destroy Operation
Prisoner of War
May 1, 1951–August 1953
The Caves

The Beginning: World War II, 1943

In 1943 Wilfred was bumming around California looking for something to do. He found it at a Navy recruiting office. At the age of 17, and with his parents' consent, Wilfred joined. He served in World War II as a gunner on a three-inch and five-inch gun. Then in 1946 he was discharged. After that he tried various jobs, but somehow civilian life just wasn't the same. That all changed shortly after the invasion of South Korea on June 25, 1950. Wilfred, now 21, walked into the recruiting office and joined the U.S. Army.

Korea: The First Assignment, March 1951

After Wilfred completed his training, he was sent to Japan with the 24th Division. There he was transferred to the 2nd Division, and a short time later he found himself standing on Korean soil. He was there for only days before he got his first assignment: to seek and kill the enemy. "We were on what we called a killer operation," Wilfred explained.

We marched for days looking for the Chinese. We found some on a few hills and we attacked them but there weren't that many. What we didn't know

150

Wilfred Ruff as a young soldier.

was that they were pulling their forces back and rebuilding for a big assault on us.

We marched a whole day and night to get to this one hill. Just a couple hundred yards away from us were the Chinese. We watched them build up their forces. We could see them and they could see us. We were just waiting for them. We were told to stand fast, but then at the last minute, for some reason or other, we were told to get out.

I'll always remember this. It took us about 30 days to dig in on this hill, with bunkers and all, and when that order came it took us about five minutes to get out.

The order came just minutes before 2:00 A.M. Then, all at once, these Chinese came screaming toward us, and of course we had to get up and start firing with everything we had. Our men were evacuating, and I was told to stay behind and cover them.

The Chinese liked to scream when they attacked. Make lots of noise. They were blowing bugles, blowing whistles, and screaming at the tops of their lungs. There must have been 300,000 of them, and there were only 30,000 or maybe 35,000 of us. But that's the way it always was. They had the men, we had the ammunition.

Wilfred was dressed in fatigues and helmet, carrying an M-1 with five bandoliers of ammunition, a .45 automatic side gun with extra rounds, a .30 caliber light machine gun with extra ammunition, and five or six grenades.

A second lieutenant came up and told me to stay behind. He stayed with me, but I don't know what ever happened to him. We were pretty close, but he was young and scared. This was his first war. It was my second.

He told me I had to get rid of 40 boxes of .30 caliber ammunition we had up there. Lots of ammo, 250 rounds in a box. I told him it took us a month to get it up here and now I have to get rid of it in less than five minutes.

There was a big hole we used as a bunker. We jumped out of our machine gun hole and took those boxes of ammo and almost filled that big hole up.

I dropped a grenade in and dived for cover. It was like a small war in there.

We had to skedaddle then too, and that's when the second looie and I split up. In the chaos he got separated from me. We left our positions, and I heard erratic gunfire. There were thousands and thousands of them coming up through a valley.

We had trip flares out there, so when one of them tripped a wire a flare would fly up into the air illuminating the area.

Being a machine gunner, I opened up on them. They were well trained, though. When that flare went off they just stood still hoping you wouldn't see them.

They kept coming. Acres and acres of Chinese. Thousands of bodies swarming toward us. All the Chinese had was lots of bodies and they used those bodies, like ammunition. Hell. You couldn't shoot them all.

By the time I got to the gully I could see these hand grenades come rolling down toward me. I figured it was our troops throwing and rolling those grenades down, as they came from our side. You could see the fuses burning on them. They were the older kind. One of them exploded so close to my ears that I couldn't hear for an hour.

We had a hard time of it. There were several other men with me by this time. We didn't know where we were, but after an hour we stumbled onto this streambed.

This Chinese soldier came up with a burp gun and started firing. There was a Mexican ahead of me, and he fired back. The Chinaman fell, and the Mexican figured he'd killed him. But he made the mistake of going up to the body to see if he had really killed him.

That's when the Chinese man opened up on him and shot the Mexican. We fired and got the hell out of there.

I got rid of all my gear: the C-rations, blanket, gear, grenades, and half of the ammunition. Later I got rid of my machine gun, but I jammed the bolt with mud and stones. The .45 caliber pistol and the remaining bandoliers of ammo were gone. Pretty soon all I had left was my M-1 with no ammo. It seems pretty funny now, but it wasn't then.

The Capture: May 1, 1951

It was just before dawn. Wilfred and the other 700 men in the area with him were surrounded, and they were out of ammo. The terrifying reality of their fate hit home: they had no choice but to surrender. "We were taken prisoner. About 700 of us were captured that morning," Wilfred recalled. "A lot of us were in the 2nd Division and some from the 24th Division." It was a dark moment for them all.

The Death March: May 1, 1951–June 9, 1951

"They marched us for about 40 days," Wilfred stated.

I didn't know how far that was in miles because nothing was in a straight line in Korea. It's a small but rugged little country. Some of the men were wounded and couldn't march. They were just shot along the way. If anybody faked an illness, they were shot too.

Others died of illness or a combination of illness and wounds. The Communists just let them die. There was no medical care.

Most of them died of dysentery. Mucus and blood waste just running down their pant legs, if they were standing. A sorry sight. A real sorry sight.

The water was bad, and so was the food. They fed us dried sorghum or millet, and they made a fish soup. Beat the fish up, brains and eyeballs and everything, and served it to us. They didn't waste a scrap.

I got dysentery after eating a handful of raw corn. It was a mistake you make and I made it. But when you're starving, you're really not that particular. I was fortunate in two ways. First, because the Chinese decided to take a break at a North Korean village near the Yalu River. We stayed four or five days in this village resting, and it was during three of those days that I had dysentery. If I had gotten it while we were on the march I would have died. Second, because a fellow soldier took care of me. You know, when you have dysentery, it's just a lot of diarrhea, the fluids just melting out of the body. I lay on my back and didn't even bother to take my pants down. This little guy, a prisoner just like I was, took it upon himself to care for me. If he hadn't cared for me like he did, I would not have pulled through.

He found me a blanket and covered me up. He took food and jammed it into my mouth. He made sure I would swallow so that after the worst was over what little food he fed me would give my body some strength.

In a couple of days, thanks to his help, I was better and ready to march again. After we reached our first camp, we split up. Got separated. I never saw this little short fellow again. He went to a different camp than mine. I heard later that he'd turned Communist, supposedly collaborated with the enemy. I don't care. I don't care what he did. He saved my life.

We moved across the Yalu River into a Manchurian prison camp. There were only 250 of us left.

Camp One: June 1951

"Life didn't get any better," Wilfred continued.

Frigid weather, beatings, torture, and dried scraps of food took their toll.

After three, four, or five weeks in the camp we got used to the sorghum and millet. We started getting a little rice too. You could say they were feeding us a little better. The few of us who had made it through survived and our wounds healed up.

Meanwhile, the temperature dipped to 30 and 40 degrees below zero. Our clothing remained thin and ragged. We were down to skin and bones. We couldn't lie on our sides because our hips were sticking out too far from malnutrition.

I felt grubby. Soap and water were uncommon luxuries. The guards let us take a bath when they felt like it. They felt like it once every seven or eight months, and they put everyone into one tub. We took turns with the bar of soap and used the same water. Steadily it got darker and darker. What I remember most is the scum at the bottom. We were so dirty that it built up fast. We kept skimming it off. I guess we got clean. Cleaner than we were before we took the bath.

Christmas was approaching and that was a break for Wilfred and the other prisoners because the Chinese were planning a Christmas party—not really because they cared about the prisoners, but rather for propaganda. Nevertheless, better conditions, if only for the short term, were better than none. "They had a propaganda deal going," Wilfred explained.

They were always going for this propaganda crap. Calling us "warmongering capitalists" and the like. So they were going to show the whole world how good they were to us.

They had their cameras going and had us line up at these indoor camp tables. They had little candy, little hard Chinese candy for us. They gave us an extra ration of rice too. On occasion they fed us dog but there were no dogs to eat. For this Christmas, little slivers of pork in some soupy stuff. I'm not sure what it was.

A lot of us hard-nosed ones said we shouldn't go in there and be a part of their propaganda movie. But what the hell, we were starving. We got something out of it, though. Once we got in line we gave them the Roman finger. A nice gesture. They could stick it you know where.

The Indoctrination: A Reactionary. "They wanted us to spout the crap they fed us," Wilfred said.

We were the capitalist warmongers. Capitalist pigs. Slaves of Wall Street. That sort of thing. If you played along, you were treated better. I refused to play along.

The Chinese had classes every day, and they started right after they got us up at 5:30 A.M.

The only English words they knew were "wakey, wakey."

We'd attend to our daily needs, then go to these classes. We had paper and pencil and were told to write our views on Communism.

I jotted my views down. I said it was all crap, a bunch of Communist jargon. I asked for more food, and all my petition did was to piss them off.

We were only getting two bowls of food a day. One bowl of sorghum or millet in the morning and another one at night. We'd get our water out of that same bowl. One in the morning and one at night.

There were about 700–750 of us in the camp, but we were dying like flies. Dysentery, gangrene, untreated wounds, and poor diet were the main causes. I stuck my neck out and spoke up. I suppose the other prisoners respected me as I had been in the Second World War. I got them to sign a petition for more food.

It didn't do any good. One day this Chinese guy in charge was antagonizing me. Wanting me to stand at attention. Then stand up and then squat. Stand up, then squat. Stand up, squat.

Well, I was ornery. I was tired of his nonsense and getting all pissed off. I reached over and slapped him.

That reaction was a big mistake for Ruff.

The Cage: The Bowels of Hell. Wilfred's hard-nosed attitude, refusal to accept indoctrination and bribes, and hitting the guard caused the Chinese to label him as a reactionary in the prison camp. "I could have been shot but I wasn't. That night they came and put me in a cage," Wilfred explained.

We slept in these huts, a bunch of men to a hut to keep warm. It was night and all of us were asleep. They pulled me up and took me out so as not to disturb anybody. I thought I was going to be taken out and shot. They took me to this other shack where there was a hole, a depression in the earth at one end. They put me into a cage which was in this hole in the ground.

So there I was. I didn't know what was going to happen to me. Of course you're scared as hell. You don't know what's coming.

Straw mats were placed over the top of the cage to keep the prisoner in the dark. There was a hole in the roof of this shack, and when the sun was out the light came right through. Sometimes you could see little rays of light come in through the mat. The cage was wooden with

Sketch of Ruff dated March 1953.

slats or bars, two and one-half feet in width, four feet high, and less than six feet long. They took you out once every 24 hours to relieve yourself. That was the only opportunity I had to get up and walk around. Otherwise it was lying on my back, cramped up in the cage. They came at night, and you tried to delay your body functions until then. The guard would stand right by you with a gun while you squatted and did your business in the field. Then it was back to the cage.

I didn't try to escape. You couldn't take off anyway. For the most part we were Caucasians in an Asian country. We were weak, diseased, with scabs all over from picking off the body lice. We were hungry. I lost 80 pounds and my normal weight was 180. Quite a few tried to escape, but they never made it.

Punishment was designed to keep light out of the cages. Sunshine and daylight can pep up a prisoner's spirits, keeping the slimmest of survival hopes alive. If you gave up you died.

I spent seven of my 28 months of captivity lying in solitary confinement in the cage. It could drive you crazy. How did I keep from going goofy? Well, I don't know. A lot of prisoners did go nuts.

I amused myself. I would pick a fly off my clothing, for instance, and use a thread to try and tie it around the fly's leg. Make a pet out of it. Since my cage was stuck in the ground I had lots of moles to play with. I tried to make pets of them too. Give them names. Anything to pass the time.

The cage was too small for you to stretch out. You had to lie cramped all the time.

The first morning that I woke up I was greeted by a Chinese interrogator. I was brought out of the hole, out of the cage. They put me in the middle of the shack and had me squat down. Squat down right where the sun could come into my eyes through the little hole in the roof.

While I was squatting under the pinpoint of sunlight, an interpreter came in and sat at this table. Sat right in front of me smoking a cigarette and blowing the smoke down into my face.

He was tapping this table, real Hollywood style too, like he was something special. I'm 25 and this is my second war and this little shit is sitting there thinking he's some kind of a hero or something.

He asked me my name. He asked me about my home. About my mother and my father. He knew I had no brothers or sisters. He knew everything about my home and about me.

"You are the last of the Ruffs," the interrogator said.

He asked me, "How does it feel to be the last of the Ruffs?"

He said, "Just remember, Wilfred, you're the only Ruff left."

He was trying to scare me. As if to say that after I was dead there would be no more Ruffs. He kept this up for a while. Then it ended, and they put me back in the box. I never saw that silly little shit again.

It didn't matter, though, because one of his buddies took his place. My cage was in the ground, but there was an opening or space on all four sides so that the guards could approach us. This one guard was a mean SOB. He would come up to me, point his gun at my head, smile, and pull the trigger. Naturally the chamber was empty. He did this to me a lot. The first time was the scariest, of course. But you never knew if there was bullet meant for you in the chamber or not. He got a kick out of trying to scare the hell out of you.

Well, one day I was in the cage as usual, lying there in the cold and damp, curled up and thinking of family and home. I thought a lot about family and home in that cage. Lots of time for such thoughts. He came down and got close to the cage. Started to give me orders. Telling me to cross my arms, put my legs together, and lie at attention. He got close enough to pinch my cheek and laugh. Taunting me.

He got close once too often. I got my hands through the bars and grabbed his neck and squeezed. I wanted to choke him to death. I held on as best I could, but he was outside the cage and able to maneuver, able to get out of my grip and get away.

He got away and brought back a bunch of my buddies.

They had these wooden rods, and they stood around me and started poking me everywhere they could. From the top, the sides, the front, and the back.

The first thing I did was cover my face with my hands, but I still got a real bad bruise over my right eye. I got a good beating. They aimed for my groin, my ribs. Got me in the arms and legs, wherever they could. They didn't break any bones, so if there was anything to be thankful for, I could be thankful for that.

Then, after poking me with the poles for about five minutes, they left.

I never did see that little guy again, but I suppose he could have been killed.

Repatriation

After that incident Wilfred noticed that the Chinese guards' behavior seemed to change. The harassment and torture stopped. Wilfred wasn't complaining, but he didn't understand. What he didn't know was that some 200 miles away at Panmunjom armistice talks were going on and an exchange of prisoners was being arranged. The agreement was close, and the Chinese were cleaning up their act in the treatment of prisoners. "They moved me out of my underground cage where I had been kept for seven months," Wilfred said.

I was put on a truck with a few other guys. Of course, it was at night. We drove a few hours and ended up in another camp where they put me into a compound with 14 other guys. We were behind a stockade fence about eight or nine feet tall. A guard walked around it.

Our bathroom was a slit trench or hole with two boards across it. You did your duty freestyle.

Outside the stockade were other prisoners. They were better fed, and we got to watch them play volleyball.

Every once in a while, one of them would come by and toss a little package of smoking material wrapped in rice paper. It was marijuana. It grew wild over there, and when the other prisoners went out on wood detail, they picked all they could. Let me tell you, that helped keep us alive.

I haven't touched that stuff since I got back from the war, but I sure used it over there. All of us did.

As we smoked it we looked to the skies. That's how we knew the war was coming to an end. We didn't see any dog fights in the air anymore.

Our planes and theirs used to fly over every day and blast away at each other. Interesting to watch. They'd fire at each other, then turn miles and miles away to get at each other again and fire again as they passed. Naturally we cheered for our pilots. But for three or four days we didn't see any action, and we knew the end of the war was near.

Besides, they started feeding us better too.

This improved diet wasn't much better than in former captive years. Besides the other ailments, dysentery still plagued us. It's loose bowel movement. Every prisoner had it. You never get over it. The poor food or no food, or contaminated food then all the parasites, worms, and insects that get into your body. My medical record shows it as "scarred walls of the intestines from parasites." That's just a nice way to say you have got the runs.

When the end was really close, they put us in another truck. We rode two days and two nights and ended up near Panmunjom. We spent a week there before our first and last ride through Freedom Gates. The Chinese had given us these blue uniforms to wear. As we drove south to our release, we began peeling the clothes off. The cap, the shirt, the pants, the shoes. By the time we were in friendly hands, we were in a pair of shorts that looked like flour sacks.

On the south side we were greeted by ladies from the International Red Cross. The ladies paid little attention to our wear as they provided us with doughnuts and coffee. But that little feast was too much for our stomachs. We were all sick from the rich food.

We were taken to another camp where we got showers and a haircut. They issued us clothes. We were told welcome back, and that was about it. Hell, they didn't even shake our hands.

I imagine the first group that got released got the band and the parades and all that crap. We were among the last to be released. We were "the reactionaries, the incorrigibles." We got nothing.

The Trip Home: August 1953

Within days Wilfred and his fellow prisoners were packed on a troop ship with regular GIs. If there was anger with his enemy, it soon carried over to his fellow soldiers.

We were crowded into bunks three decks high. We didn't want special treatment, but we did want some people to use common sense.

We prisoners had been on a diet of millet or sorghum for two to three years. I was down to 100 pounds. Everybody was thin and weak. Now they put us on a crowded ship and tell us to eat what the regular GIs ate. The regular GIs were eating rich stuff like meat and spaghetti and spaghetti with spaghetti sauce. We couldn't eat that. We were upchucking it all the way across the Pacific Ocean.

The regular troops couldn't understand that. They laughed at us a lot. There was talk. As weak as we were, we got into fights with them.

What the hell, most of the troops on that ship were punchy young kids who hadn't seen any fighting.

Relief came when the ship hit San Francisco's harbor.

A Father's Search in San Francisco: September 1953

I tried to make up for the 28 months of prison life in two days and nights. Before I got off the ship the government gave me $250. I wasn't a married man, and you better believe I was going to spend all $250.

My father, John, came out from the Midwest to get me and take me back home. I forgot to mention to my dad where I was going when I got off the ship.

I met a cab driver who asked me where I wanted to go, and I said anywhere he wanted to take me. He knew of a place that I might like, so he made me a deal. He would forget about the meter on the cab if I would pay for the booze.

We went to this joint where you could buy a lot of cheap whiskey. It was a place where you couldn't see the windows or the doors once inside. The women came around to sit on the tables that you were at. We forgot about time when we got inside.

Meanwhile my father was on the streets of San Francisco searching for his son. He had the whole San Francisco Police Department looking for me. He found me in the bar. We reunited, then crossed the Rockies and the Great Plains, arriving in Chicago in September.

Home Sweet Home: September–October 1953

Wilfred arrived home to reminisce with his family. He was thinner, but gained 20 pounds with his mom's home cooking. He and his old girlfriend, Pat

Mullen, who had waited for his return from the war, were reintroduced. On October 31, 1953, Pat became Mrs. Wilfred Ruff.

The New Assignment

All was not well, however, when he received his new assignment at Fort Sheridan. "They had promised me a position as a recruiting sergeant, as we were usually allowed to pick a job coming back as prisoners of war," Wilfred explained.

> But that was not the case with Korea. It was the war that everyone wanted to forget, and they didn't care about us.
>
> They found out I had been in the military police at one time, and so they decided to make me a security sergeant near Great Lakes at Fort Sheridan. They put me in this old stone building that had been built during the Civil War. It could hold up to 75 prisoners. Now that was a hell of a place to put a guy who had just been in a North Korean prison camp.

Ruff took his frustration out on a prisoner who smarted off, calling him Wilfred this, Wilfred that. He told him to shut up, but when the man didn't, he locked all 145 pounds on his challenging enemy.

Finally, in 1954 Wilfred was honorably discharged from the U.S. Army.

The Aftermath: The Spring of 1954

It was spring 1954, and the war and prison camp were behind Wilfred. He was starting a new life. Most if not all that life would be spent with Pat, the childhood sweetheart he married on Halloween of 1953.

On one occasion, they were walking arm in arm on a sidewalk from their apartment on Chicago's north side to the neighborhood Riviera movie theater at Broadway and Lawrence. Wilfred doesn't remember what was playing that day. Popular movies at the time included Alfred Hitchcock's *Dial M for Murder*, *The Robe*, in Cinemascope, *How to Marry a Millionaire* and *From Here to Eternity*, with Marilyn Monroe, and *Prisoner of War*.

The couple wasn't alone. Other couples were out for a Sunday afternoon stroll, on their way to the movies, a baseball game, or perhaps to the corner drugstore for a Coke float.

A jet flew over, breaking the sound barrier with a loud boom.

"All of a sudden I'm down on my knees," Mrs. Ruff explained.

> Will's down on his knees right beside me. He pulled both of us down. We're lying there on the sidewalk with all these people staring at us. I'm embarrassed. Don't know what's going on. It happened so fast.

POW Recognition Day at the Illinois governor's mansion. Will Ruff sits in the foreground at right; his wife, Pat, looks over his shoulder.

I whispered to Will, asked him what was wrong. He said to forget it. It was nothing. So we got up as if nothing had happened and walked to the show.

I found out later he was used to being strafed by American jets in the prison camps. The American pilots couldn't always distinguish a prison from a military encampment.

For years to come, when Wilfred remembered, he would drink to forget. It helped some, but nothing would ever let him completely forget the encounters with death, the beatings, and the terror in the compounds.

Epilogue: Life in 1997

There are few things working right in Wilfred's body today. His limbs suffer from arthritis, his feet still react to cold, his knees are shaped by shrapnel, and parasite scars help form the walls of his intestines. He blames his poor health on the 28 months of exposure, confinement, and starvation while imprisoned.

"It was always cold," Wilfred stated. "Summer came on a weekend in July, arriving on Saturday and leaving on Sunday."

Wilfred is a light sleeper. "He'll hear a noise and he'll get up. Jump right out of bed," Mrs. Ruff said.

Today Wilfred and Pat live on a hill above the Fox River in Algonquin, Illinois. They are surrounded by five children, their spouses, and five grandchildren. In a more heroic age, Wilfred's resistance to the enemy would have warranted recognition as a hero. But in a mediocre age, after the war, he returned home to silence. "The Korean War was the forgotten war," Wilfred said. The government just wanted to forget about us." That statement is true, but regardless of what the government wanted to forget, his family has not. In their eyes he is a hero, to those who know about sacrifice he is a hero, and Wilfred is just proud of having served his country.

APPENDIX A:
TEMPORARY PRISON CAMPS

Practically all the POWs captured between November 1950 and January 1951 spent some time in at least one of several temporary camps set up by the Chinese. Some POWs were there only two or three days, while others spent three or four months in the camps. The main three camps were located in valleys: Valley, Death Valley, and Peaceful Valley.

In these camps life was little more than a struggle for survival. A considerable amount of time was spent looking for firewood, but other than burial details, there was little required of the prisoners in the way of work. What little energy they possessed was devoted to staying alive.

Housing was primitive and crowded. During the first few weeks, because there were no eating utensils, the POWs ate out of tin cans or their hats turned inside out.

Valley

Valley was organized in November 1950 and was under North Korean jurisdiction until December, when the Chinese took control. It was mostly populated by the 1st Cavalry Division, captured at Unsan during the first week of November. At its peak, more than 1,000 POWs were interned here. When the prisoners were moved, 500–700 of the 1,000 had died.

Death Valley

Death Valley was organized in December 1950 and was divided into an upper camp, which consisted of South Korean POWs, and a lower camp which consisted of UN prisoners. At the peak there were 2,000 POWs, of whom only 1,200 survived.

163

Peaceful Valley

This camp was opened in December 1950, and POWs captured at the Chosin Reservoir were held here and subjected to intensive interrogation. This camp was closed in March 1951. Approximately 1,900 prisoners went through this camp, and it is reported that 500 of them died.

Mine Camp, Mining Camp, and Soup Camp

"Mine," "Mining," and "Soup" camps were names given by Americans to other temporary camps located southeast of Pyongyang near Suan. The death rate was high in these camps also. One report stated that at one camp there were about 1,000 prisoners and three weeks later 250 of them had died from dysentery, pneumonia, and starvation.

Appendix B: POW Camps
in North Korea

This is a list of specific prisoner of war camps, their locations in North Korea, and general information about the camp conditions and operations. The material was obtained from an army document titled *US POWs in the Korean War— A Study of Their Treatment and Handling by the North Korean Army and the Chinese Communist Forces.*

Camp One

Established: March 1951–August 1953

Location: At the village of Changsong, the camp was located in the valley of the Yongji River approximately five miles from where it flows into an estuary of the Yalu, and less than ten miles from the Yalu River itself.

Prison population: 1,400 lower-ranked men; Companies 1 through 4 were U.S. personnel, while Companies 5 through 7 were composed of British POWs. The U.S. and British prisoners were housed at opposite ends of the camp from each other. Initially, about 2,000 British and U.S. officers and enlisted men were housed in this camp, but by 1952 the officers and a number of other enlisted prisoners were moved. When the prisoners were repatriated, Camp One had the largest number of POWs: 900 U.S. and 500 British.

Security: Approximately 200–300 Chinese guards were located at the corners of the camp. They were armed with rifles and submachine guns. A few fences were constructed around the camp. Guards were increased at night.

Conditions: The weather was 40–50 degrees below zero in the winter and very hot in the summer. There were body lice, dysentery, intestinal worms, pneumonia, night blindness, beriberi, frostbite, skin disorders, dental problems, starvation, and the constant threat of death. There was very little medical treatment.

165

Camp Two, Company 1

Established: October 1951–August 1953
Location: At P'Yongjang-ni, about four miles from the Yalu River.
Prison population: There were approximately 383 U.S. enlisted men and officers in the camp. Three-fourths of the population were officers.
Security: There were about 200 Chinese guards armed with rifles and sub-machine guns located at this camp. From six to eight guard posts were located at intervals around the fence and gates, and from four to six additional sentries were stationed on the high ground behind the camp.
Conditions: Reports by officers indicated that they witnessed no torture or beatings at this camp. However, two men who tried to escape were confined in a doorless shack in subzero weather without heat for 16 days. Men suffered frostbite. General treatment was fair except during the study periods by the Chinese.

Camp Two, Company 2

Established: October 1952–August 1953
Location: P'Yongjang-ni, about a half mile east of Camp Two, Company 1, and about 500 yards off the main road.
Prison population: Approximately 150 officers were held in this camp.
Security: The compound was surrounded by woven wire and barbed wire. During daylight hours there were approximately 100 Chinese guards who manned four guard posts in the camp. At night additional guards were posted outside the compound as a secondary perimeter.
Conditions: The conditions were the same as in Camp Two, Company 1.

Camp Two, Company 3

Established: August 1952–June 1953
Location: At Chungha-Dong, located on the banks of the Ch'ungmangang River, which flows into the Yalu River about eight miles north of Companies 1 and 2.
Prison population: About 130 American and British enlisted men were housed here who, for various reasons, had been labeled as reactionaries. When the camp was disbanded in June 1953 the POWs were sent back to one of the camps they had originally came from.
Security: Three separate barbed-wire fences were located around the compound. The 50–100 Chinese guards manned the six posts in the compound. Each guard relief did a head count on the prisoners, and at night the guards were doubled.

Conditions: Body lice, starvation, no medical treatment, isolation, beatings, beriberi, dysentery, and intestinal worms all constituted daily conditions in this camp.

Camp Two, Company 4

Established: May 1952–August 1953
Location: Sang-Dong, a few miles from Camp Two, Company 1.
Prison population: About 140–175 POWs, mainly U.S. Air Force officers, enlisted men, and a few UN officers, all captured late in the war. They were organized into three platoons.
Security: Loosely organized, this camp consisted of a number of houses in the village which had been taken over by the Chinese to house the POWs.
Conditions: Because the camp was opened late in the war, the conditions by Korean standards were good.

No Name Valley

No Name Valley was also believed to be an annex of Camp Two, but was so named because the prisoners were kept scattered throughout the valley in small isolated groups. Reports indicate that the Chinese were not planning to repatriate the Americans held in this valley. During Operation Big Switch, other POWs began to rebel against the Chinese, and in the end the Americans in the valley joined the other POWs and were sent home.

Camp Three

Established: June 1951–August 1953
Location: This camp was six miles northwest of Camp One on the banks of an estuary of the Yalu River and about six miles north from the river itself.
Prison population: This camp held approximately 870 prisoners of war. The POWs consisted of American enlisted men and officers and British enlisted men. In 1952 the camp was reorganized, and all the POWs other than American privates and corporals were send to other camps.
Security: The camp had approximately 250 Chinese guards who manned six to nine guard posts during the day. At night extra post and roving guards were added. The camp had some barbed-wire fencing, but the security was simplified because the camp was located on a point that protruded in the river.
Conditions: There were dysentery, intestinal worms, beriberi, starvation, torture, inadequate medical care, and stress from indoctrination.

Camp Four

Established: August 1952–August 1953

Location: This camp was located on the banks of the Wiwon Gang River, farther north than any other Chinese-controlled camp.

Prison population: This camp held all the sergeants except those doing hard labor in Company 3, Camp Two. There were approximately 600 POWs, mostly American, with the remainder British, Turkish, and French. The camp was divided into three companies. Each held about 200 men. Company 3 contained all the black American sergeants.

Security: This camp was surrounded by a six- to eight-foot barbed-wire fence and separated by a wall of mud and rock. The guard strength was about 250 men, with four or five guard posts and two guard towers. Additional guards were employed during the night.

Conditions: There were dysentery, intestinal worms, beriberi, starvation, torture, inadequate medical care, and stress from indoctrination.

Camp Five

Established: January 1951–August 1953

Location: In the west end of the town of Pyoktong. Koreans were removed from the west end of the town and POWs were housed in the empty huts. This was the first permanent POW camp.

Prison population: When the camp first opened, it held nearly 3,500 POWs, but the death rate was high and the number of prisoners decreased continually. Typically it held about 1,200 POWs.

Security: The camp was separated from the town by a four- or five-foot barbed-wire fence, which bisected the peninsula. The camp underwent many reorganizations, but the security remained fairly simple. Approximately 200 Chinese manned 10 to 12 posts in the camp, and an estimated 1,200–1,500 additional Chinese soldiers were located in the village of Pyoktong. These soldiers were not directly involved in the security of the camp but could be called if needed.

Conditions: This camp was known for an intense Communist indoctrination program effort. The death rate was very high. Most of the POWs resisted the indoctrination and were often tortured and beaten. Food was inadequate, consisting of hard corn and rice and beans. The prisoners had severe weight loss. The medical treatment was primitive. One POW reported that he had maggots in a wound and that a Chinese nurse burned them out. Another POW with a .45 slug in his leg didn't tell the Chinese for fear they would cut his leg off.

Camp Six

Established: March 1953–August 1953

Location: Located at Pyongyang.

Prison population: This camp held about 100 enlisted men and a few officers captured in the closing stages of the war.

Security: The Chinese had minimal guards at this camp because of the small number of POWs and the fact that the war was soon coming to an end.

Conditions: Because the war was in the late stages, the camp had good conditions by Korean standards.

Camp Seven

Established: September 1950–October 1951

Location: This camp was located at the tip of the Sino-Korean border until March 1951. At that time, the POWs were moved 12 miles southward to the site of some old Japanese barracks.

Prison population: This camp held about 600 POWs, including civilian internees at Manpo who were still under the control of the North Koreans.

Security: North Korean guards were placed at various posts to guard the prisoners.

Conditions: No camp organization was instituted by the North Koreans, who did very little to ameliorate the hardships the prisoners suffered. Conditions were primitive, and many died. In the middle of October 1951 the camp disbanded, and the prisoners still alive, about 300, were moved to other camps.

Camp Eight

This camp, located at Kangdong, had no information. Possibly it was used to house Republic of Korea soldiers, with no American POWs interned in the camp.

Camp Nine

This camp, at Pyongyang, is possibly the same camp as Pak's Death Palace (or simply Pak's Palace). It is believed that when the camps were given numbers Pak's Palace was designated Camp Nine.

Camp Ten

Established: July 1950–August 1953

Location: Ch'on-Ma was near the village of Kodsane, southward, close to the 38th parallel.

Prison population: A transit camp.

Security: A large number of Chinese guards were used for security.

Conditions: This camp was known as the "Bean Camp," because of the soybean diet, and also as the "Mining Camp," because it was near an old mine. The men who arrived in this camp—usually after a death march—were generally in poor condition. Many of these death marches ended with fewer than half of those men who had originally begun the march. The diet, cold weather, and lack of concern by the Chinese resulted in very high death rates for those in these camps. When the camp was evacuated, there were 800 prisoners in the camp. It was not reported how many of those were American.

Camp Eleven

This camp was located at Pukchin and was called Camp Kanggye. The camp was primarily used as an interrogation center. The prisoners were then shipped north to other permanent camps. The camp was closed in March 1951.

Camp Twelve

Established: February 1951–December 1951

Location: This camp was shifted from place to place, always in the vicinity of Pyoktong, until it was finally established ten miles from Pyoktong.

Prison population: The prison never held more than 80–100 POWs.

Security: The North Korean People's Army ran the prison.

Conditions: The prison was a center for the preparation of propaganda speeches and broadcasts. The Chinese Central Peace Committee was located at this camp and became the most notable there. When the camp closed down, the POWs were sent to Camp Five.

The Caves

The Caves were located near Pukchin. This series of caverns was used to hold prisoners who were considered troublemakers or to be uncooperative with the military. The prisoners had their food thrown at them, lived in unsanitary conditions, and suffered the lowest level of degradation of any prisoners in the war.

Pak's Death Palace

Pak's Death Palace, north of Pyongyang at Saun, was the main interrogation center for 30 or 40 UN troops at the time. It was also known as the "brick yard" because it was located near a brick factory. Pak was the name of the North Korean officer in charge of the interrogations; he was considered the cruelest in the war. His brutal interrogation tactics established this camp as the worst prisoner of war camp in the Korean War. Reports indicate that this camp was renamed Camp Nine.

Camp Dina Kahn

This camp was located at Andong in the apex area on the Yalu. This camp had been a military police training camp for the Japanese during World War II. A map by one prisoner indicates that there was a kitchen, a hospital, and a barber shop, which was different from other prisoner of war camps.

Camp Jungkan

This camp was also located in the apex of the Yalu. It was an old Japanese base on the top of a mountain. The camp was nicknamed "The Death Camp" because so many prisoners died there. The reports by POWs indicate that prisoners would scrape the ground for hours to make graves for the dead. In the winter the ground was frozen two feet deep. The naked corpse would be placed in the hole, with no dog tags or any markers and the guards would barely give the prisoners time to cover the bodies. When the prisoners refused to cooperate with the guards, they were taken out into the snow, forced to take their shirts off, and the guards would pour cold water down their backs.

APPENDIX C:
THE CODE OF CONDUCT

Korean prisoners of war had a markedly different experience from that of POWs in other wars. The indoctrination, or so-called brainwashing, was the first experience of this kind that U.S. prisoners of war had encountered. Although research concluded that there really wasn't any brainwashing but rather the same techniques of indoctrination that other Communist countries used, the U.S. military became concerned. In 1955, after much debate, a Code of Conduct was established which all future military personnel could be trained by and could follow in the event of captivity:

I

I am an American fighting man. I serve in the forces which guard my country and our way of life. I am prepared to give my life in their defense.

II

I will never surrender of my own free will. If in command I will never surrender my men while they still have the means to resist.

III

If I am captured I will continue to resist by all means available. I will make every effort to escape and aid others to escape. I will accept neither parole nor special favors from the enemy.

IV

If I become a prisoner of war, I will keep faith with my fellow prisoners. I will give no information or take part in any action which might be harmful to my comrades. If I am senior, I will take command. If not, I will obey the lawful orders of those appointed over me and will back them up in every way.

V

When questioned, should I become a prisoner of war, I am bound to give only my name, rank, and service number, and date of birth. I will evade answering further questions to the utmost of my ability. I will make no oral or written statements disloyal to my country and its allies or harmful to their cause.

VI

I will never forget that I am an American fighting man, responsible for my actions, and dedicated to the principles which made my country free. I will trust in my God and in the United States of America.

INDEX

175